Intro

This book was gradually written over the course of a few years. Recipes have been sourced from personal experience and tips from friends. They have been selected in mind to respect the seasonal fruit and vegetable calendar as much as possible, while maintaining influences from all over Europe and occasionally beyond. They are cheap and cheerful, having typically been created during periods of low income.

I started getting into cooking about the age of 19, as I became very curious about the food I was serving in the Alexander Hotel. Thankfully the Hungarian chef Norbee was patient in his explanations and tips. Seasonal vegetables came a few years later, as I began to search for an improvement on some of the miserable, tired-looking products which were sold in supermarkets.

A Wednesday market in Salon-de-Provence initially sparked my interest with the excellent selection of fruit and veg around the greater Marseille area. That later developed with regular visits to one closer to home in Marley Park, then at a greengrocers in Manchester and later at a massive weekly market beside the Dynamo Dresden stadium. I've always found a trip to the market like a walk through nature, as the colours of the season are on display like a natural art gallery.

Eating through the seasons further gives us reason to celebrate all times of the year. Whether that be rhubarb at the tail end of winter, pumpkin coming into autumn, or bright oranges at the darkest time of the year, there is something unique to all 4 seasons. By glamorising the less flash months, we can also avoid the curse of spending a year waiting for summer, which arguably is the macro version of being miserable all week waiting for the weekend.

Local agriculture gives us a sense of regional identity too, and supporting it gives us a sense of being a responsible customer and citizen. Food is so central to a country's culture and history, as well as to our own personal history. Who amongst us has not had a Proustian transformation back to our childhood whilst eating a strawberry at a picnic, or seeing baked beans fall into the grid of frozen potato waffles?

While this is a cookbook, I've included a soundtrack to it. Along with food, music has been a constant in my life, ever since as a young teenager I was staying up late discovering new tunes on the radio. I find that just like fruit and veg guides us through the year, radio guides us through the week. The knowledge that everyone else listening is sharing your hump-day feeling is reassuring and lends a distant, yet local, sense of community.

Music can also be a means to improve your humour. I have a distinct recollection of the opening to New Order's 'Bizarre Love Triangle' single-handedly eliminating a crippling hangover.

This moment when a tune hits is extra-ordinary, like the pang of vinegar off a fresh bag of chips. The right song heard at the right time can define a night, a city, a holiday, a year, a relationship, a break-up or a goodbye.

Music, just like food, is inseparable from where I either first sampled it, or where it had its strongest impact. I hear The Lotus Flowers and I'm transported to the after-party of a hurling tournament in springtime in Vienna. I hear James and I'm back on an indie-disco dancefloor in Manchester, arms outstretched, singing my heart out and not knowing what to do with my life. Just like when I taste a soft green fig, and my soul wanders back to the Croatian coast where I first tasted such delicate softness.

Some of these tracks belong to their season as much as asparagus to May, or the return to school to September. My hope is that these memories will last forever, kept alive by their musical associations.

Cooking and music go hand in hand when preparing food with friends and family. It forges strong links, again defined by what was cooked, what was learnt, what was discussed. An ideal social catch-up for me involves staying in, preparing some good food, with tunes, chats and czerwony wino.

So whether you're cooking for friends, filling family lunchboxes, or sorting a quick supper for yourself, I hope you find some inspiration here to get in the kitchen.

I wish you happy reading and happy cooking.

Seán x

Note on recipes

While every effort has been made to make these as understandable as possible, a few points are worth mentioning:

- Always wash fruit and vegetables
- Use your senses to guide you. If something smells burnt, take it off the heat.
- Use common sense where I have not.
- Adapt to your taste. Many of these recipes are generous with oil for example, you may gladly use a bit less.
- Ovens can be deceptive. My oven's 200c is probably not the exact heat as your oven's 200c.
- **Highlighted text** is generally given as a key tip to help you either with the recipe in question, or to employ this technique elsewhere.

Index:

July Recipes:
- Stewed Peaches and Yoghurt
- Cherry-Stuffed Croissants
- Mixed Herb Omelette
- Green Beans in Tomato Sauce

August Recipes:
- Peach and Cardamon Chutney
- Sweetcorn and Courgette Fritters
- Fennel, Seaweed and Artichoke Paella
- Cauliflower in Spiced Tomato Sauce

September Recipes:
- Aubergine, Tomato, Mozzarella Bake
- Broccoli Orzo and Buttery Chard, with Tomato Salsa
- Tofush and Chips
- Apple Cake

October Recipes:
- Courgette Tagliatelle
- Potato Soup
- Mushrooms on Toast
- Gnocchi in Cheese Sauce with Kale Salad

November Recipes:
- Leek, Goat's Cheese and Thyme Risotto
- Lemon and Garlic Potatoes
- Quick Courgette Quiche
- Kale, Gorgonzola and Walnut Pasta

December Recipes:
- Mushroom and Lentil Ragù with Polenta
- Vegetable Crisps
- Smashing Pumpkin Soup
- Pasta with Chickpeas and Brown Bread

January

January is the grimmest month. Wet socks, the wind hitting that top bit of your chest between your shirt and your jacket, continental soccer on a winter break, and inane newspaper articles about sticking to your new year's resolutions.

The comfort of the indoors is the best way to turn a positive spin on this. Let the windows steam up from the simmering pasta sauce, treat fat as an insulation, find something escapist to read, and descend (ascend?) into your own universe.

Root veg are not the only source of nutrition during this time; apples, squash, and your store cupboard will help you through these long thirty-one days.

In this month of darkness, take shelter inside and slow things down. Rather than the sound of prosecco popping, seek some dark and soft music to light a candle to.

- Joy Division : Atmosphere
- Teho Teardo and Blixa Bargeld : A Quiet Life
- Trembling Blue Stars : My Face for the World to See
- Ride : Vapour Trail

January recipes:

- Leek and Potato Soup
- Salsify and Hazelnut Pasta
- Beetroot, Walnut and Feta Risotto
- Soda Bread

Leek and Potato Soup

A smart cooking technique takes away the need to add lashings of butter and cream to this soup. Feel free to treble the caramelised onions and reserve 2/3 in a sterilised jar. This griddling of the leeks gives a nice smoky taste and can be incorporated into other recipes, or brought into a salad with buckwheat, rocket and cubed cheddar.

Ingredients (4 starter portions):

- 2 large leeks
- 2 medium onions
- 4 cloves garlic
- 3 tbsp brown sugar
- 4 tbsp white or cider vinegar
- 4 medium potatoes
- 2 tbsp mustard seeds
- 1 litre veg stock
- 4 tbsp rapeseed oil
- Parsley or dill, to garnish

Recipe:

- Peel and finely chop the onions. Cook in a pot on low heat with a pinch of salt and 2tbsp rapeseed oil for 10+ minutes. Peel the garlic and remove the bitter green stalk from the middle (if applicable). Slice the garlic in thin batons and add to the pot for 3 mins. Add the sugar and vinegar, and leave to simmer for another 10 minutes, until it's a bit of a jammy consistency. Add mustard seeds.
- Heat the vegetable stock. Peel the potatoes, chop into cubes of 3cm, rinse and add them, along with the stock and simmer until cooked through, likely about 7-8 minutes. Don't use all the stock immediately. **With liquid, you can always add more, but you can never take it back.**
- Meanwhile, heat up a griddle pan, or a grill, or a George Foreman. Top and tail the leeks (remove most of the green end and only the 'hairy' white end), slice lengthwise in half and rinse under running water. Add 2tbsp rapeseed oil to the pan, then griddle the leeks for 3-4 mins each side on a high heat until slightly blackened. Season with salt and pepper.
- Remove the leeks, slice into 3cm chunks and add to the pot. Blitz with a blender, check the seasoning and add the parsley or dill.
- Serve in a bowl with a drizzle of rapeseed oil and some bread on the side.

Salsify and Hazelnut Pasta

Unknown and underappreciated. This outsider vegetable is coming into your kitchen to shake up the established order. Can be found in jars in France and Germany at least, a possible shortcut.

Ingredients (4 light main courses):

- 400-500g salsify
- 400g penne
- 4 cloves garlic
- 120g hazelnuts
- 1 lemon
- 6 tbsp olive oil
- 1tsp chilli flakes
- 1tbsp dried thyme
- Parmesan to grate over

Recipe:

- Salsify needs a tough washing, then peeling. Your chopping board will get dirty during this process. When peeled, rinse again thoroughly and chop into 5 cm lengths. **If leaving unattended, you'll need to put them in a bowl of water with a bit of vinegar or lemon juice to stop them discolouring.**

- Put a pot of water on the boil and heat a frying pan to medium.
- Toast the hazelnuts in the dry pan, tossing them around the pan for 1 min until they turn a darker brown and can be clearly smelt. Remove from the pan and shake between hands to remove extra skin.
- Add 4tbsp of the oil to the pan, then fry the salsify in it until starting to colour (ca. 5 mins) then drop the heat and add chopped garlic, chilli flakes and thyme. Continue to cook over a low heat until the salsify can be pierced easily with a knife, probably another 4 minutes. Add grated lemon zest and its juice directly into the pan. You may want to add the rest of the oil if it's looking a bit dry. **As there's no strict liquidy sauce here, you're relying on a mix of oil and pasta cooking water to make it a bit more fluid.**
- Meanwhile, cook pasta in a pot of salted water according to packet instructions. Drain, reserving a small cup of cooking water.
- Add pasta to the salsify pan, along with a splash of the cooking water (or as much is needed) in order to get a slight liquid coating.
- Add the parmesan, check seasoning and serve with some extra olive oil and parmesan available for guests.

Beetroot, Walnut and Feta Risotto

Fresh is best* (see note below), but a good quality ready-beetroot can turn this into an achievable Tuesday night supper.

Ingredients (4 main courses):

- 4 medium, or 2 large beetroot
- 400g risotto rice
- 1 medium onion
- 1 small carrot
- ½ a celery stick
- 4 cloves garlic
- 120g hazelnuts
- 200g feta cheese
- 150ml white wine
- 1+ litre veg stock, kept hot
- Olive oil, rapeseed oil or butter
- Juice of half a lemon
- 4 tbsp fresh parsley
- Parmesan (optional)

Recipe:

- If using fresh beetroot, rinse briefly, then top and tail (i.e. trim off the very top and the very bottom). Wrap the beetroot in tinfoil and roast in a preheated oven at around 180c until soft inside. This can also be done the day before while something else is roasting, as this can take up to an hour, depending on the beetroot's size. When cooked, allow to cool before peeling and slicing into bitesize chunks.

- If using jarred beetroot (sold as 340g usually?), drain the liquid from the jar.
- **Prepare the soffrito**: Peel the onion and chop roughly. Peel the garlic and slice into thin batons. In a pot on a low heat, add 2-3 tbsp oil (or butter), then the diced onion and cook for 5 minutes. Meanwhile, chop the carrot and celery into similarly sized pieces to the onion. Next, add the carrot, celery and garlic with a pinch of salt and pepper. If the pan is too dry you can add another tbsp of oil here. **Cover and leave to soften for 10-15 mins**. That amount of time is necessary to soften the vegetables thoroughly. **This technique is typically used as the base for many soups and stews.**
- Increase the heat to medium, then add the rice along with a tbsp of oil (or butter) and mix it around for 1 minute to toast. Add the white wine and let it bubble away while you get a whack off the boiling alcohol. Drop the heat to low once you can no longer smell raw alcohol.
- The veg stock should be kept hot throughout. So either mix a cube with boiling water, or if using fresh stock, heat it up in another pot. Gradually add some stock every few minutes (or as the mix starts to dry out) and stir gently. The aim is that there is always just enough hot stock covering the rice. Continue to do so until the rice is cooked. This may take 20 mins or even more, depending on the rice used.

- Meanwhile, toast the hazelnut pieces in a dry pan on medium heat for 1 minute until you can smell them and they're beginning to darken in colour.
- When all is cooked, add the beetroot. Cube the feta roughly and add in, along with the toasted hazelnuts and parsley (can substitute other earthy, leafy herbs, such as chervil or dill). Add an extra glug of oil or a knob of butter in, squeeze in the lemon juice, cover and leave to the side for 5-10 mins.
- Serve in bowls with side salad, with grated parmesan if using.

*Beetroot tops can be cooked like chard. Fry the stalks in olive oil on a medium heat for 3 mins, add some garlic for 2 mins, then the leaves for 1 minute. Can be served as a side dish for the risotto.

Soda Bread

Slight variations are available on this recipe with what you want to throw in the mix. I almost always tend to burn the raisins, so I'd advise keeping an eye on this during the latter stages of cooking. A multi-function measuring jar is ideal for all sorts of baking.

Ingredients:

- 250g white flour
- 250g brown flour
- 100g oats
- 1 tsp baking powder
- 1 large carrot or medium courgette
- 50g rapeseed oil
- Pinch of salt
- 1 large handful of seeds/nuts/fruit of choice
- 400-500ml **buttermilk***

Recipe:

- Preheat the oven to 170c
- Grate the veg of choice into a large bowl
- Measure the flours, oats, baking powder and add to bowl, along with seeds of choice, oil and salt
- Mix and make a well in the bowl. Add initially 400ml of the liquid (you may not need all of it), and mix together with a wooden spoon. When stirred, the mix should move around the bowl smoothly as one 'springy' block.
- Sprinkle some flour on a lined baking tray, dump the mix onto the tray and flatten it out a bit with the spoon. Cut a cross into the top of the bread and put in the oven for about 25-30 mins. Keep an eye in the latter stages that the raisins don't burn. You can check it's done by taking the bread out and knocking on the underside – it should make a hollow sound.
- When finished, leave to cool somewhat before storing in a cotton bag and/or with kitchen paper wrapped around it. Should last up to 4 days like this.

*Buttermilk, or alternatively slightly gone-off milk, or milk with a splash of vinegar added. Non-dairy options also possible.

February

February is the disappointing sequel to January. Hopes of an improvement in temperature are usually short lived, and things tend to get worse before they get better.

The kitchen as a source of warmth continues. Other sources of optimism include a decrease in the frequency of writing the wrong year down when signing a date on something, the school holidays towards the end of the month and the return of the Uefa Cup.

Darkness progresses gradually into light in February. The sun sets about 90 seconds later each day, so there is a noticeable change between the beginning and the end of the month, both in the sky and in our humour.

Think of roasting veg, cooking a grain and some kind of purée and/or cheese for a bulky lunchbox. Roasting recommendations are available in the fried feta recipe below.

As the most significant date of the month is Valentine's Day, here are a couple of songs for the occasion:

- The Smiths: There is a Light That Never Goes Out
- Jane Birkin et Serge Gainsbourg : Je T'Aime
- Billy Bragg : Valentine's Day Is Over
- Devinyls : I Touch Myself

- **February Recipes:**
- Parsnip Soup
- Tagine
- Cauliflower and Black Olive Pasta
- Fried Feta with Roast Veg and Spelt

Parsnip Soup

Roasting the parsnips brings out their best, and if you roast extra, they can be used in a winter salad with some blue cheese, green leaves and nuts. To bulk out this soup further, you could add about 100g red lentils to the pot. Cook them in vegetable stock and add the parsnips/garlic at the very end before blending.

Ingredients (Serves 4):

- 750g parsnips
- 1 large onion
- 1 medium potato, peeled
- 6 cloves garlic
- 1 stick celery
- 1 small carrot
- 1-2 tbsp vinegar (optional)
- 1 litre veg stock
- Rapeseed oil
- Salt, pepper

Recipe:

- Preheat oven to 220c.
- Peel, dice finely and soften the onions in 2 tbsp oil in a pot on a low heat for 10+ minutes. The onions should be softening gently. Add a touch of salt to aid the process.
- Chop the potato, carrots and celery into small chunks. Add all 3 to the pot and continue the low cooking for another 5 minutes.
- Wash and chop the parsnips into lengths.
- **Roasting Tip: Aim to chop the parsnips into wedges, so the cooked edges vary from slightly burnt to soft.**
- Cover a roasting dish with greaseproof paper. Lightly crush the garlic cloves with the side of a knife, then toss them in whole with the parsnips into the roasting dish. Season with salt and pepper, and add 2-3 tbsp rapeseed oil, then roast until cooked as to the above description, about 20 minutes.
- Heat the vegetable stock. Once the parsnips are ready, remove the skins from the garlic. Add the garlic flesh, along with the cooked parsnips to the pot, add the vegetable stock and simmer all together for 2 minutes.
- Blend. Check the seasoning and add the vinegar if to your taste.
- Serve with some warm buttered bread.

Tunisian Winter Stew

North African stew which can have its spice enhanced with extra cumin or chilli. Quantities can easily be doubled. Merci à Hédi pour m'en avoir conseillé.

Ingredients (Serves 4):

- 2 onions
- 4 cloves garlic
- 4+ tbsp olive oil
- 2 large carrots
- 1 large parsnip
- 1 handful of winter greens*
- 400g can chopped tomatoes
- 400g can chickpeas, rinsed
- 4 tbsp chopped ginger
- Salt, pepper
- 4 tbsp cumin seeds
- 4 tbsp coriander leaves
- 4 tbsp ras-el-hanout
- 1 tsp cinnamon
- 1 tbsp honey
- A squeeze of tomato paste
- 2 large handfuls of chopped dates, dried apricots or sultanas

- In a large pot, heat 4tbsp of olive oil on a low heat. Peel and finely dice the onions and garlic, then add to the pot.

- Cover the pot for 7-8 mins and continue cooking until the onions start to become soft. Add the seasonings (a few grinds of salt and pepper, plus ca. 4tbsp each of cumin, coriander and ras-el-hanout, plus 1 tsp cinnamon) and the chopped ginger, and toss so that the onions are coated in the spice mix. Continue to soften for another 2 mins.
- Chop the carrots and parsnip into discs about 1cm thick, discarding the top end of the veg. Add the carrots and parsnip to the pot and stir into the spices for 1 minute while continuing the cooking.
- Add the chopped tomatoes with tomato paste and about half the empty tomato tin of boiling water. Heat up to a simmer and leave cooking for 10 mins, until the veg starts to soften.
- Remove any stalk from the greens, then chop or tear the leaves roughly. Rinse them thoroughly, as dirt often gets trapped within.
- Drain the can of chickpeas. Add the chickpeas and greens to the pot, along with the honey and fruit of choice. You can add 2 handfuls of one of the fruits or a mix of all of them as you wish. Simmer on a low heat for at least another 3-4 mins, although a longer slow cook will not damage the dish at all.
- Check the seasoning and adjust as necessary.
- Serve with couscous**, yoghurt and flatbread.

*Examples of winter greens include green cabbage, chard and kale. This recipe is easily adjusted in other seasons to include squash, courgette, aubergine...any veg that can soak up the flavours of the tagine mix.

**Couscous can be easily personalised by adding either turmeric before the boiling water with butter after, or adding lemon juice and pomegranate seeds after it is cooked. In both cases, use some extra olive oil to loosen it and fluff it out.

Black Olive and Cauliflower Pasta

Sicilian Winter pasta dish from my former housemate Fede. A parallel recipe can be made using broccoli and green olives in place of the cauli and black.

Ingredients (Serves 4):

- ½ a large cauliflower
- 150g black olives*
- 4 cloves garlic
- 1 red chilli
- 1 lemon
- 400g pasta of choice
- Grated parmesan (optional)
- Olive oil
- 2 tbsp oregano
- Salt, pepper
- Salad and bread, to serve.

- Break cauliflower into small florets, as they are naturally formed. Cut some of the larger ones in half. Any leftover stalk can be chopped into 1/2cm cubes. Rinse thoroughly in a colander.
- Boil salted water in a pot. Add cauliflower for 60 seconds, then put the cauliflower into a bowl using a slotted spoon and set aside. Keep the water for cooking the pasta later.
- Peel and thinly slice the garlic. Remove the stalk and seeds from the chilli and chop it finely. Remove the pits from the olives.
- In a frying pan on a low heat, heat enough olive oil to cover the base fully, about 4tbsp. Add the olives, along with the diced garlic and chilli, oregano, and grate the zest of the lemon directly into the pan. Infuse this together by cooking on a very low heat for 10 mins.
- **Add the cauliflower pieces, along with a splash of their cooking water. Stir together and cover the pan with a plate (or greaseproof paper or tin foil). Cook on a low heat for up to 20 mins. The idea is that the cauliflower partially roasts and partially steams.** Once a knife passes through the thickest cauliflower piece easily, the mix is ready.
- Cook the pasta as per packet instructions.
- Mash the cauliflower mix when done with a potato masher, add lemon juice, cheese (if using), another glug of olive oil (optional) and pasta, along with another splash of the cooking water to achieve a more sauce-like consistency.
- Serve with a mixed salad and some bread on the side.

Fried Feta with Roast Veg

Born out of necessity, this was made during a Lidl-based food-shortage where the halloumi shelf was empty. The roast veg are ideal for a lunchbox, when combined with a grain of choice (spelt, couscous etc).

Ingredients (Serves 2, with snacking leftovers):

- **Fried Feta:**
- 250g feta
- 1 egg
- 4 tbsp flour
- 6 tbsp breadcrumbs
- Sunflower oil
- Salt, pepper

- **Roast Veg:**
- 1 large courgette
- 2 peppers
- 2 medium potatoes
- 3 tomatoes
- 1 large red onion
- 3 cloves garlic
- Olive oil
- Salt, pepper
- 2 bay leaves, 4 slices of lemon, chilli flakes and oregano to taste

- **Recipe:**
- Preheat the oven to 220c.
- Wash, prepare and chop the veg as appropriate: Top and tail the courgettes, remove the stalk and seeds from the pepper, remove any gone off bits from the potatoes, remove the hard core from the tomato, top, tail and peel the onion. Slice the potatoes and onions thinly, and the other veg can be chopped more roughly.
- Crush the garlic cloves with the side blade of a knife, add with the veg onto a roasting tray, along with about 4tbsp olive oil, the bay leaves, lemon slices and seasoning.
- **Don't overcrowd the tray as that will delay the cooking time.** The veg should not be stacked onto a second 'layer'.
- Roast for 30-40 mins, until char lines appear on the veg. Switch oven off.
- Meanwhile, beat the egg, then arrange the flour (seasoned lightly with salt and pepper), beaten egg and breadcrumbs in 3 separate bowls. Heat 4-5 tbsp of sunflower oil in a frying pan on a medium-high heat. Slice the feta into thick strips (aim for 6 from a block).
- Dip the feta strips in the flour, egg, breadcrumbs in this order, then fry, turning a minimum in the pan (the feta's structure may be quite fragile). Only turn over once, once they are lightly browned underneath.
- Serve with the roasted veg, and some salad and grains of your choice.

March

The 'Return of the Jedi' of the early year winter trilogy. The death star of cold, rainy weather continues, and the people's only hope is the outbreak of a rebellious bout of 15 degrees sunshine.

Annoyingly, the switch between winter and spring can make you a bit under the weather. Look after yourself here. Plenty of garlic and chilli helps against a cold. Soup season simmers on.

To mark the arrival of the weekend, take the time on a Saturday morning to have a proper breakfast. Cheese omelette or scrambled eggs. Add a spoon or two of natural yoghurt to give the eggs a lighter touch. The more disciplined of you will know that abstinence from excess on Friday night is the key to a happy and refreshing weekend.

While all roads lead to spring, St Patrick's Day claims the middle of the month. Here are some lesser known Irish indie gems.

- Fight Like Apes: Captain A-Bomb
- The Wonder Villains : Ferrari
- Whipping Boy : We Don't Need Nobody Else
- Republic of Loose : Comeback Girl

March Recipes:

- Wild Garlic Pesto
- Turnip Greens
- Red Lentil Soup
- Rhubarb Crumble
-

Wild Garlic Pesto

Possible to get foraged, if you have the right guide/knowledge. Double or treble the quantities if you wish. This format works with plenty of other greens. Even a mix of carrot leaves and rocket produces something very satisfactory, just add an extra bit of garlic to balance everytrhing.

Ingredients (1 medium and one mini jar):

- 1 medium bunch wild garlic leaves (or 150g other green leaves)
- 1 small lemon
- 6 tbsp walnuts
- 4 tbsp grated parmesan
- Chilli flakes, pepper
- 100+ml olive oil

Recipe:

- In a blender (small, fast version, not the handheld one), blend the walnuts, cheese and some grinds of pepper and chilli flakes with a splash of water.
- Add the juice of half the lemon, along with 100ml olive oil. Blend again.
- Rinse and add the wild garlic (or whichever leaves you're using), then blend very briefly, until just mixed.
- Taste the mix, and judge whether you need to add more cheese, lemon juice or oil for flavour, or another couple of splashes of water for consistency.
- Seal in disinfected jars* finishing with a layer of olive oil on top and store in a cool, dry place (on opening, store in the fridge).

*A thorough wash with soapy hot water, followed with clear hot water, then again with cold water, before being left to dry will do the job here. To be even more diligent, you can dry the jars afterwards in an oven on a very low heat (50c).

Turnip Greens

A case of one veg providing three different ingredients, akin to St Patrick's explanation of the shamrock. Turnips, stalks and leaves are cooked in this order to produce a fine side dish. Add some ricotta and bread to bulk it into a lunch. The same format also works perfectly with baby beetroot.

Ingredients (2 light lunches):

- 1 bunch of baby turnips with tops and leaves attached (usually 3-5 in a bunch)
- 1 small lemon
- 4 tbsp sunflower seeds
- 2 cloves garlic
- Chilli flakes, salt, pepper
- Rapeseed oil

Recipe:

- Rinse the turnips under running water. Cut the baby turnip bulbs off from the stalks. Cut the squiggly end off each turnip. Cut each bulb in half, then slice each half into ½ cm slices.
- Heat a frying pan to medium-high. Add a glug of oil (about 2 tbsp) to the pan and begin to fry the turnips, tossing around the pan as you go for 3 or 4 minutes.
- Peel and slice the garlic into thin slices, then add to the pan, along with some chilli flakes, salt and pepper to your taste.
- Cut the stalks of the turnips into 1 cm pieces, throw into the pan and continue cooking for another minute.
- Chop the leaves up roughly and add into the pan, cook for another minute.
- Switch the heat off, grate lemon zest directly into the pan and squeeze the lemon juice in too. Check the seasoning and serve.

Red Lentil Soup

Pleasantly versatile with either Mediterranean or curry spices.

Ingredients (4 starter portions):

- 1 large onion
- 1 carrot
- 1 stick celery
- 1 medium potato
- 1 pepper (optional)
- 6 cloves of garlic
- 2 large red chillis
- 250g red lentils
- 1 can of chopped tomatoes
- 1 veg stock cube
- 2 tbsp tomato purée
- 1 tbsp vinegar (optional)
- Oil (olive if Mediterranean, sunflower if curry), salt, pepper

- Mediterranean seasoning: oregano, thyme, fennel seeds

- Curry seasoning: cumin, coriander leaves, ginger, turmeric, garam masala

Recipe:

- Peel and chop finely the onions and garlic, chop the carrot, celery and pepper (if using – remove stalk and seeds) into 1cm pieces. Chop the chilli finely, removing the seeds for a milder heat.
- Heat a large pot to a medium-low heat, then soften the vegetables in it with a generous glug of oil (about 4 tbsp) for 7-10 minutes. Add the garlic, chilli and seasonings* of choice (Mediterranean or curry) and cook for another 3 minutes.
- ***add about 1 tbsp of each spice or herb. When you stir it in to the mix, you should be able to lightly smell its impact on the dish.**
- Peel the potato, chop into 1cm pieces and rinse briefly under running water. Add to the pot and stir into the mix.
- Mix the veg stock cube into boiling water as per packet instructions.
- Rinse the red lentils, then add them to the pot along with enough veg stock to comfortably cover them. Simmer for 10 minutes, until they're almost tender. You may need to add more stock if they begin to dry out.
- Add the can of chopped tomatoes, rinse the remainder of the tin out with a splash of water and add the tomato purée. Allow to bubble for another 5-10 minutes.

- Stir thoroughly to combine. Add the vinegar if using. Check the seasoning and adjust as necessary.
- Serve with a drizzle of oil, some yoghurt and some bread.

Rhubarb Crumble

A classic desert to mark the onset of spring. Oats and müsli give added nutrients. Any excess of stewed fruit can be refrigerated for breakfast with some yoghurt.

Ingredients (Serves 8):

- 2 bunches of rhubarb (1kg total)*
- 2 tbsp chopped ginger
- 1 large orange
- 120g brown sugar
- 120g flour
- 120g butter + extra cubes to top up
- 120g+ müsli
- 100g chopped almonds

Recipe:

- Preheat the oven to 190c. Trim the ends of the rhubarb, and chop into 3cm chunks. Put in a roasting dish (one that'll be suited for the whole crumble) with a splash of water. Roast for 15-20 minutes, or until mashable.
- When done, mash the rhubarb and add the chopped ginger. Grate the orange zest in directly and squeeze in the orange's juice, along with 2 tbsp of the sugar to taste. **It should still taste sharp, and will ultimately contrast with the sweet topping.**
- For the crumble topping, in a large bowl mix with your hands: flour, butter, the remaining sugar, müsli, chopped almonds. **The topping needs to cover all the rhubarb, so if it's a bit thin, just add a little more müsli, butter, sugar and flour and remix.**
- Once the quantity is ok, spoon atop the crumble and dot with a few small cubes of butter.
- Bake in the preheated oven for 20-30 mins, until the crumble has a crispy/crunchy texture and is beginning to lightly brown.
- Serve with greek yoghurt, ice cream or warm custard.

*Change fruits as per the season: peach, plum, apple etc..
Ginger is not a must for these, it simply complements the rhubarb nicely.

April

April is where things really start to pick up. Yes, it may rain a fair bit, but the clocks changing and a new bout of evening daylight have a massively positive effect on the soul.

From here to maybe September, there's a feeling that we do not want to look forward to anything, but just enjoy the moments of the everyday. A long Easter weekend allows us to recognise what is genuinely important in life.

Try incorporate something into each day which you actually want to do. Culinarily, this may include an undisturbed moment with a cup of coffee, an obscene amount of cheese on pasta, or a packet of crisps with a beer and some soccer on TV.

Spring is in its early stages, without quite massively hitting us yet. Don't begrudge the rain from providing us with the lively, verdant landscape.

- Jesus and Mary Chain : April Skies
- Garbage : Happy When it Rains
- Stone Roses : Waterfall
- Basement Jaxx : Raindrops

April Recipes:

- Spanokopita
- Peppers and Pasta
- Pan Haggerty
- Halloumi with Salads

<u>Spanokopita</u>

Beautiful with some raw tomatoes and/or radishes. After putting this much effort into a dish, keep the side dish as simple as possible. Spinach and kale can be replaced with other greens as you see fit. Filo pastry could improve this, but that would mean extra preparation.

Ingredients (serves 4):

- 375g shortcrust pastry
- 2 medium red onions
- 4 cloves garlic
- 200g spinach
- 200g kale
- 250g feta
- 1 courgette
- 1 lemon
- 2 eggs
- 2 tbsp oats

- 1tbsp chilli flakes
- 1 tbsp oregano
- 4 tbsp milk
- 4 tbsp sesame seeds
- Salt, pepper
- Olive oil

Recipe:

- Preheat the oven to 200 degrees.
- Peel and finely chop the onions and garlic, before softening in a pot on a low heat with 3-4tbsp olive oil, chilli flakes (according to taste), and a generous amount of oregano, salt and pepper.
- Remove the stalks from the kale. Rinse, then roughly tear up the leaves. Add them to the pot.
- Rinse the spinach thoroughly in a colander. Roughly tear up and add to the pot along with **the oats (these soak up any excess liquid).** Stir continuously until fully wilted.
- Top and tail the courgette and grate it all into the pot. Stir for another minute, then taste the mix and adjust the seasoning as necessary. Switch off the heat.
- Beat the 2 eggs into the pot and stir through.

- Spread the pastry out onto a lined baking tray (the packets usually come with a cut piece of baking paper). Cut some excess off and reserve.
- Top with the spinach mix, cube the feta and add it in, along with the zest and juice of the lemon. Stir it around so it's evenly distributed.
- With the remaining pastry, cut 1cm thin strips from it, and use these to line over the tart in diagonals.
- Brush the entire tart with some milk (pastry brush is best for this, although you can use your hands if necessary), and sprinkle with sesame seeds.
- Bake in the oven for 25-30 minutes, checking as you go along that it doesn't get too brown. If the top is getting dark brown, cover the tart with tinfoil or greaseproof paper and drop the heat to 180c before continuing.
- Remove from the oven and allow cool slightly for 10 minutes before cutting into portions.
- Serve warm with a simple, cool salad.

Peppers and Pasta

Quick and reliable. Be particular about the olives you get. Ones with stones in are routinely better.

Ingredients (serves 2):

- 200g short pasta (penne, fusilli etc)
- 1 red pepper
- 2 yellow peppers
- 3 cloves garlic
- 1 large tomato
- 50g black olives
- 1 tbsp tomato purée (optional)
- 1 tbsp red wine vinegar
- Chilli flakes, tarragon
- Salt, pepper
- Parmesan
- Olive oil

Recipe:

- Boil the pasta in salted water according to packet instructions.
- Prepare the peppers. Remove the stalk and seeds, then slice into lengths 1cm thick.
- Heat 3tbsp olive oil in a frying pan to a medium-high heat.

- Sauté the peppers in the pan until they start to blacken somewhat. Add sprinklings of chilli, tarragon and pepper to your taste (but no salt or just a spare amount – the olives do this for you).
- Peel and slice the garlic into thin strips. Drop the heat to low and add these to the pan for 1 minute.
- Chop the tomato finely (removing the core) and add in with the tomato purée (if using), plus a splash of water. Continue cooking for 2 minutes.
- Remove the stones from the olives, add the de-stoned olives to the mix along with the vinegar. Stir gently and continue cooking for another 2-3 minutes.
- **Drain the cooked pasta, reserving a half cup of cooking water. Add some of the water to the pan, stir to loosen up. The aim is to get a slightly thick, yet liquidy sauce which will coat the pasta. Neither watery nor a solid block, but somewhere fluidly in between.**
- Add the pasta to the pan. Stir to coat.
- Serve with some green leaves, a grate of parmesan and a drizzle of olive oil.

Pan Haggerty

Hailing from the unlikely culinary capital of Newcastle, this dish is perfect for when the rain is tapping all evening on your window. Something green and palate cleansing would accompany this well, although for a full Northumbrian experience, serve with a side of Pease Pudding and a bottle of Brown Ale.

Ingredients (serves 2):

- 6 medium potatoes
- 3 medium onions
- 100g strong cheddar
- 2 tbsp mustard seeds (optional)
- 1 handful mixed seeds
- Salt, pepper
- Vinegar
- Rapeseed oil

Recipe:

- Wash the potatoes and slice them thinly lengthwise, then rinse again. Pat the potatoes dry with kitchen paper.
- Peel and slice the onion into thin strips. Boil some water in the kettle.
- Heat 4tbsp of oil in a pan to a medium-high heat, then fry the potato slices with a pinch of salt, pepper and the mustard seeds, trying to cover all with the oil and seasonings. Continue until lightly browned.
- Add the onion strips. Once they begin to colour, drop the heat to low, add the grated cheese, a splash of vinegar, a splash of boiling water, then stir around and cover with a plate (or foil, or greaseproof paper). Continue cooking for another 5 minutes. **The idea is that a light layer of liquid on the bottom is steaming the mix.**
- According to taste, you may add more oil or vinegar or seasonings here. When the cheese has melted and the potatoes are cooked through, add the mixed seeds and divide onto 2 plates with your side serving of choice.

Halloumi with Salads

This is designed to be as easy as possible in preparation; it's the main course I would choose if I was a contestant on Come Dine With Me. The couscous and potatoes can be prepared in advance and served warm or at room temperature. You could leave one of them out & replace it with a chopped baguette for an even easier option.

Ingredients (serves 4):

- halloumi, 800g

For the salad:
- 1 small head of lettuce
- 2 ripe tomatoes
- 1 small cucumber
- A few slices of jarred beetroot
- 1 handful nuts and/or seeds
- Olive oil, vinegar, salt, pepper

For the couscous salad:
- 250g couscous
- 3 tbsp raisins
- 3 tbsp dried apricots (or dates or other dried fruit)
- 2 tbsp tomato paste
- 1 small lemon
- 1 courgette
- 1 carrot
- 2 tbsp veg stock powder (or 1 stock cube)
- Small bunch of coriander (4-6tbsp chopped) (optional)
- Olive oil

For the potato salad:
- 500g new potatoes
- 4 cloves garlic
- 2 tbsp capers
- 150g rocket
- Small bunch of mint (4-6 tbsp chopped)
- 4 tbsp butter
- Olive oil, salt, pepper

Recipe:
- Salad: Rinse the vegetables, cut into small pieces, and toss in a bowl with the dressing ingredients (about 2tbsp oil, 1tbsp vinegar and a grinding of salt and pepper)

- Couscous: Combine couscous, raisins, dried fruit, tomato paste and the veg stock powder in a large bowl. Pour over boiling water to submerge it slightly, then cover with a plate for 8 mins until the water is absorbed. Grate the courgette and carrot directly in, grate lemon zest in and squeeze its juice in, add a couple tbsp olive oil and the fresh coriander and fluff everything up together with a fork.

- Potatoes: Cook the potatoes in salted water until just about cooked through, you want them to maintain their structure. Drain and put aside. Peel and chop the garlic into thin batons. Heat 2 tbsp oil and the 4tbsp butter in a pan, then cook the garlic for 1 minute on medium heat. Add the capers, rocket and mint, along with a grinding of salt and pepper. Add the potatoes back in and stir through.

- Griddle or fry the halloumi in a small amount of olive oil until charred on both sides.
- Serve each dish in its own bowl or plate, and let the guests compose their own meals.

May

May is my favourite month. In no other time of the year is there such a feeling of optimism in the air. The blossom and the longer evenings transmit themselves into our souls, and there's a positivity echoing throughout society. The feeling of the now dominates, and for a while we are no longer counting down days till some future event.

Now is indeed a time to slow things down significantly. Presently writing from Germany, the extended series of bank holidays is something we should all aspire to. Finland however tops the EU poll with 15 public holidays, another victory for Scandinavian progression.

The time to enjoy the outdoors kicks off here too. Depending on where you are, this may be urgent as the heat could get too high in the following months. Cycle to work, or at least take your bike out on shorter journeys. Find a nearby place to eat lunch outside.

A further beauty of this time of year is the end of soccer seasons, with promotion and relegation being decided under blue skies and bright sunshine. Not to mention European Cup finals, and the Eurovision. Don't expect any indie hits from the latter, just allow yourself to shamelessly enjoy the Eurodance and Turbo Folk on offer, and don't take yourself too seriously.

- Malcolm McLaren : Madame Butterfly
- The Darling Buds : If I Said
- Sash : La Primavera
- The Undertones : Here Comes the Summer

May Recipes:

- Green Asparagus
- Asparagus and Pea Purée
- Cauliflower, New Potato and Cheddar Quiche
- Sausages in Tomato Sauce

Green Asparagus

A celebration of the season. Can be mixed into pasta, served as a side, put into an omelette, risotto, a baguette etc.

Ingredients (serves 2 as a main, 4 as a side):

- 500g green asparagus
- 3 cloves garlic
- 1 lemon
- Pepper, salt
- Olive oil or rapeseed oil

Recipe:

- Wash the asparagus. Snap off the hard bit at the end of each stalk, as in the attached photo. The main part of the stalks will probably weigh just about 350g at this stage. Reserve the hard ends in a bowl for another recipe (see Asparagus and Pea Purée). Toss the stalks in 2 tbsp oil.
- Peel and slice the garlic thinly. Heat a griddle pan (or a frying pan) to a medium high heat. Cook the asparagus on each side until beginning to char, likely about 4 minutes each side. Drop the heat to low. Add the garlic and another tbsp of oil if the pan is drying out. Continue to cook on a

low heat for 3 minutes, or until the garlic is fragrant and slightly coloured.

- Grate the lemon zest directly into the pan. Switch off the heat. Squeeze in the lemon juice, watching out for any pips. Season and serve in dish of choice.

Asparagus and Pea Purée

A versatile dip which can also be used as a pasta sauce or a sandwich filler. Also ideal on slices of a baguette with a litte cube of feta on top. If you have any leftover whole cooked asparagus you can put it in the blender to increase the quantity.

Ingredients (4 snack portions):

- Broken tips from 500g asparagus (likely about 150g in weight)
- 2 cloves garlic
- ½ a lemon
- Pepper, salt
- 2+ tbsp olive oil or rapeseed oil
- 200g frozen peas
- 1 handful sunflower seeds
- Parmesan to taste (optional)

Recipe:

- Peel and chop the garlic roughly. Put the garlic into a blender with the juice of the lemon, oil and a pinch of salt and pepper.
- Meanwhile, bring a small pot of salted water to the boil. Trim the external very ends (half a centimetre) off the asparagus tips and discard. Cut the asparagus lengths in half.
- Put the asparagus pieces in the boiling water. Once they are close to being cooked (about 7 or 8 minutes probably), put the peas in with them for another 3 minutes. Drain.
- Put the vegetables into the blender with the garlicky oil and blend until puréed.
- Check the seasoning, add parmesan if using and blend again. Taste and see if it needs anything. Serve in a bowl with the seeds scattered over.
- **Tastes of nothing? Add lemon juice and some salt. Too thick? Add some water. Too flat? Add pepper.**
- Aim to use within 2-3 days.

Cauliflower, New Potato and Cheddar Quiche

Perfect for a picnic, or simply to have something to lazily pick at after work on a Monday. First a thin slice, then just a wee cube where there's a strong concentration of cheddar..

Ingredients (serves 4):

- 375g shortcrust pastry
- Half a medium cauliflower
- 2 cloves garlic
- 1 onion
- 250g new potatoes
- 200g strong cheddar
- 5-7 eggs (size depending)
- 3 tbsp natural yoghurt
- 3 tbsp milk
- 3 tbsp wholegrain mustard
- Pepper, salt
- Rapeseed oil

Recipe:

- Preheat the oven to 190 degrees.
- Peel and finely chop the onion and garlic. Heat 2 tbsp of oil in a frying pan on a medium-low heat. Cook the onion and garlic in the pan until softened, about 7-10 minutes. Season with salt and pepper, then put in a large bowl.

- Chop any larger baby potatoes into 2 and break the cauliflower into its naturally forming florets. Any remaining stalk of the cauliflower can be cut into 1cm cubes.
- Rinse the potatoes and cauliflower. The potatoes don't need to be peeled, just remove any off-looking bits. In a pot of salted boiling water, cook the potatoes. Once cooked, remove and let cool slightly.
- In the same pot, cook the cauliflower for 2 minutes until only partially cooked.
- Add the potatoes to the onion/garlic bowl along with the cauliflower florets. Chop the cheddar into small cubes and add to the bowl, along with the mustard.
- Line a big enough oven dish (this was 23x23x8cm) with greaseproof paper. Roll out the pastry and line it evenly into the dish. Any excess pastry can be cut off and reserved for some pastry lines on top of the quiche.
- Crack the eggs into the bowl one by one, beat together with the other ingredients, plus give an extra seasoning of salt and pepper. You may get away with using one egg less. Add the yoghurt.
- Pour the mix into the pastry-lined dish. Top with some extra pastry lines if you have them.
- Using a pastry brush (or failing that, just your fingers), brush the milk onto the exposed bits of pastry.
- Bake in the oven until a knife poked into the centre comes out clean, bearing in mind that a longer, flatter dish (ca. 20

minutes cooking) will cook through quicker than a shorter, deeper one (ca. 40 minutes).
- Remove from the oven and allow to cool down slightly before serving with salad, bread or accompaniments of your choice.

Sausages in Tomato Sauce

Get familiar with what's good in terms of 'meat-style' products where you are, there can be a huge gulf in quality. This dish is ideal eaten room temperature as part of a picnic spread, but can also be enjoyed as a complete evening meal.

Ingredients (serves 2 as main, 4 as side):

- 350g veggie sausages of choice (or 4 large sausages)
- 1 large red pepper
- 4 cloves garlic
- 1 red onion
- 1 handful black olives
- 4 medium tomatoes
- 2 tbsp tomato paste
- 1 tbsp vinegar
- Chilli flakes, oregano, pepper, salt
- Olive oil

Recipe:

- Heat 1 tbsp olive oil in a frying pan to medium high. Brown the sausages all over and continue cooking for another 2-3 minutes. Remove the sausages.
- Chop the pepper into thick strips and fry in the same pan until beginning to blacken. Remove.
- Peel and finely chop the onion and garlic. Cook both in the same pan over a low heat until softened, adding another tbsp of oil to the pan if the pan is too dry. Season with sprinklings of salt, pepper, chilli and oregano, according to your taste.
- Remove the core from the tomatoes. Chop the tomatoes roughly and add them to the pan and increase the heat slightly. Cook through for about 10 minutes until the tomatoes start to become a sauce.
- Destone the olives and discard the stones. Add the tomato purée, vinegar and olives to the pan.
- Chop the sausages into 2cm pieces. Continue cooking the sauce for a few minutes more, adding a splash of water if it's not looking 'saucy' enough, then drop the heat, add the sausages and peppers and check the seasoning.
- Let the dish cool down somewhat before serving, either with salad, cheese and bread, or with picnic accompaniments of your choice.

June

In Ireland June starts with the Leaving Certificate, and radio shows are filled with people ringing in with memories of being ill-prepared for Maths, Geography, or French, due to a rare outbreak of gorgeous weather or an even rarer Irish participation in an international soccer tournament.

Memorisation is a central part to exam success in Ireland, and quotes from W.B. Yeats still portray an image of spring/summer tranquillity in my mind; "Lake water lapping", "Nine bee rows will I have there, a hive for the honey bee". Staying with Irish literature, Bloomsday occurs in the middle of the month. Leopold Bloom stops in Davy Byrne's pub for a glass of burgundy and a gorgonzola sandwich, a tribute to which can be found in this month's recipes.

Hopefully agreeable weather will grace your June and you can enjoy discovering the pockets of nature dotted around your city. Catch the sun shining on a small, insolent patch of green, surrounded by obedient concrete.

Pay attention to your nearest fruit and veg shop/market, some gems can appear from June onwards. Things like gooseberries for jam, or peaches, nectarines and apricots. Enjoy these fruits, along with the increased availability of local tomatoes, radishes and cucumbers. Preparing a meal is a lot easier with quality produce, and more so when instead of applying heat to everything, you can simply add olive oil, vinegar, salt and pepper.

- Marth and The Vandellas : Dancing in the Street
- The Lotus Eaters : First Pictures of You
- The Hold Steady : Constructive Summer
- Arab Strap : The First Big Weekend

June Recipes:

- Strawberry and Leek Salad
- Battered Courgettes
- Crudités and Dips
- Melanzane Sandwich

Strawberry and Leek Salad

Something of a show-off for a picnic. Any incorporation of fruit into savoury dishes really brings a 'wow' factor to the table, with minimal effort. Could be a simple lunch with bread and ricotta.

Ingredients (serves 4 as a side):

- 3 medium leeks
- 250g strawberries
- 1 handful walnuts pieces
- 1 tbsp vinegar
- 2 tbsp fresh tarragon or basil
- Pepper, salt
- Olive oil or rapeseed oil

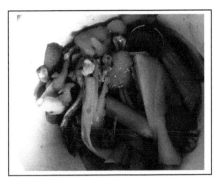

Recipe:

- Heat up a griddle pan to a high heat, or alternatively a George Foreman grill or a frying pan.
- Toast the walnuts for about 1 minute until you can smell them, then remove and put in a large bowl.
- Top and tail the leeks, and slice lengthwise in half. Rinse thoroughly as bits of grit tend to get trapped within. When clean, chop each length into sections about 5cm long.

- Add 2 tbsp oil to the pan, then griddle the leeks for 4 mins each side on a high heat. **They should be charring on the outside; a small bit of blackness is desired, as it carries a certain flavour.** Season with salt and pepper. Put in a bowl to the side to cool.
- Wash, hull and slice the strawberries thickly, add to the bowl.
- Tear the basil or tarragon, add in along with 1tbsp oil and 1tbsp vinegar, stir, then check the seasoning by tasting the juices at the bottom. Serve at room temperature.

Battered Courgettes

A somewhat lighter version of a childhood chipper favourite. If you have leftover batter, feel free to experiment with other fillings. Papa Silvio would be proud.

Ingredients (serves 4 as a starter):

- 6-8 small courgettes
- 100g flour
- A bottle of beer
- Salt, pepper,
- 2 tbsp fennel seeds
- Sunflower oil
- 2 lemons

Recipe:

- In a bowl, season the flour with a generous grinding of salt, pepper and 2 tbsp fennel seeds. **Make a well in the middle and gradually pour and stir the beer in. You'll likely need between 100 and 150ml. The final consistency should resemble natural yoghurt.** Fridge it for 30 mins.
- Drink the rest of the beer.
- Top and tail the courgettes, then slice thinly lengthways (about half a centimetre). Put them into another bowl and season lightly with salt.
- Heat up a frying pan to a high heat. Thinly cover the base of the pan with sunflower oil, then allow it to heat up for about 30 seconds.
- Remove the batter from the fridge, then dip the courgettes into it, then fry each side in the pan. Will likely take 30 seconds each side, but check until they're oh-so-lightly browned.
- Put the cooked courgettes onto plates lined with kitchen paper.
- Continue cooking the courgettes in this manner, adding more oil to the pan as necessary.
- Chop the lemons in half. Serve the courgettes on a platter with the lemon slices at each corner.

Crudités and Dips

Another uncomplicated early summer lunch. You'll notice the improvement in quality by sourcing some local veg from a market or a good greengrocer. Make a bit more as needed, as the leftovers fit in fine for a sandwich to bring to work the next day.

Ingredients (judge depending on how many are eating):

Crudités:

- Carrots
- 1 Cucumber
- 1 Red and/or yellow pepper
- Radishes
- ½ a Cauliflower (optional)
- Pepper, salt
- Lemon juice
- Olive oil or rapeseed oil

Dips:
- Hummus
- Cream cheese
- White bean dip
- Guacamole

Recipe:

- Wash all the veg. Slice the carrot, cucumber and peppers into batons. The cauliflower can be sliced into small florets, and the radish into slices. Main thing is that they're 'dippable' in structure.
- Lay the veg out on a platter or in a bowl. Scatter over some salt and pepper, then very lightly drizzle with oil and add a squeeze of lemon juice.

The dips can be either shop-bought or home-made. Following options:

Hummus – Blend 1 drained can of chickpeas with 2 tbsp tahini (or peanut butter at a stretch), 1 chopped clove of garlic, 4 tbsp olive oil, the juice of 1 medium lemon and your herbs/spices of choice (e.g. cumin, coriander, sumac). Can be further customised by adding some cubed beetroot or roasted red pepper slices blended into the mix.

Cream Cheese – Heat 1 litre of full-fat milk up to a simmer. Add 2 tbsp of lemon juice, reduce the heat to low. Continue cooking until the curd and whey* separate from each other. The curd looks a bit like cream cheese, the whey is the leftover liquid which looks like stained milk-water.

Place the curds into a cheesecloth (coffee filter paper or kitchen paper over a sieve also works) and allow the liquid to drain into a bowl, while occasionally softly pressing it through. Put the white cheese into a bowl. Season the cheese and serve.

*don't discard the leftover liquid. It's tasty in baking or even for cooking grains in.

White Bean Dip – Gently soften 2 cloves peeled, chopped garlic and a few leaves of sage (or 1tbsp dried sage) in 3tbsp olive oil in a pot. Add 1 drained can of white beans (e.g. cannellini). Heat through, add lemon juice, a splash of water, season with salt and pepper, then mash together.

Guacamole – Cup 2 ripe avocados open and remove the stones. In a bowl, leave 1 finely chopped clove of garlic in 2 tbsp lemon or lime juice for a few minutes to soften its rawness. Add the avocado in and mash together. You can also add 1 finely chopped tomato to bulk it out cheaply. Season and add coriander leaves.

Melanzane Sandwich

More elaborate than Leopold Bloom's lunch, this comes from lunches had in The Pig and Heifer on Dublin's South Quays during a time spent working off Townsend Street. Do as they do, serve it with buttered pasta.

Ingredients (serves 2):

- 1 large aubergine*
- 2 large soft sandwich baps
- 1 handful walnut halves
- 100g gorgonzola
- 1 tomato
- ½ a red pepper
- 1 handful rocket
- 2 tbsp runny honey
- Pepper, salt
- Red wine vinegar
- Olive oil
- Buttered cooked pasta, to serve

Recipe:

- Heat up a griddle pan to a high heat. Toast the walnuts for 1 minute until you can smell them, then remove and put in a large bowl.

- Top and tail the aubergine and cut into lengths, about half a centimetre thick.
- Add 2 tbsp olive oil to the pan, then cook the aubergine slices through on both sides (they can also be roasted in the oven). Once cooked, place on a plate and allow cool while you continue with the rest.
- Remove the core from the tomato and the stalk and seeds from the pepper. Chop the tomato and red pepper into 1cm cubes, and mix in a bowl with the rocket, walnuts, and a seasoning of salt, pepper, 1tbsp olive oil and a splash of vinegar.
- Optional: Preheat the oven to 180c.
- Assemble the sandwiches: Stuff each bap with the salad mix, then the aubergines, then the gorgonzola on top.
- Optional: Put in the oven for a few minutes to allow the cheese to melt.
- Mandatory: Put a drizzle of honey on top of the gorgonzola.
- Serve with cooked pasta tossed in butter. **(This in general is a great sandwich accompaniment, very useful for using up the mixed ends of a couple of packets).**

*To save effort on cooking the aubergine, you can chop up some slices from a jar of marinated aubergines and put them in the sandwich. While they may be pricy in a fancy deli, a cheaper, yet great quality version is usually available at Bulgarian or Romanian shops.

July

July sees the summer develop itself and sometimes makes us feel as we're in a foreign land. Those who spent the last 8 months complaining of the cold and dark now find the opportunity to redirect their anger towards the sun and its associated evils.

True however, that an issue I have always found with this period of mid-summer is that there can be a sense of ennui due to the inactivity of this period, as the days and weeks are no longer as clearly structured. July is a relaxed month in the kitchen too, so unsurprisingly most of this month's recipes have a minimal preparation time. It won't be until the later stages in August when we notice the temperatures descending once again, so it's highly beneficial for the soul to push oneself to get outdoors and feel the season (the same could be said for any month I guess).

Parallel to the change of working routine, the sport calendar also offers us a break from the norm. Wimbledon, Tour de France, Uefa Cup qualifiers (perfect for geography lessons as you price St Patricks Athletic's potential away trip to Torpedo Kutaisi) and even cricket take on a new appeal. No surprise that all of them involve the spectators lounging in the sun with a drink in hand. Make sure you do likewise this month.

- Kraftwerk: Tour de France
- Booker T and the MGs : Soul Limbo
- Bran Van 3000 : Drinking in L.A.
- Los Planetas : Que Puedo Hacer

July Recipes:

- Stewed Peaches and Yoghurt
- Cherry-Stuffed Croissants
- Mixed Herb Omelette
- Green Beans in Tomato Sauce

Stewed Peaches and Yoghurt

A breakfast I was fortunate enough to devour every morning during a work trip to Malta. Adjust the quantities per person.

Ingredients (per person):

- 2 medium peaches
- 1 tbsp brown sugar
- 150g greek yoghurt
- 4 tbsp of granola
- Dusting of cinnamon (optional)

Recipe:

- Heat up a pot to a medium heat. Cut the peaches into quarters, remove the stone. Simmer the peaches with the sugar and a splash of water for 5-7 minutes until softened through.
- Serve in a bowl with the yoghurt, granola and the cinnamon sprinkled on top.

Cherry-Stuffed Croissants

This was a favourite of mine in a previous hotel job where I could get the leftover croissants from the morning's breakfast. Also a fine way to use your spoils from the supermarket bakery's reduced section. Late Night Tesco Hunters, or the 19:30 Club at Marks and Sparks.

Ingredients (Serves 2):

- 2 almond croissants
- 16 cherries
- 4 tbsp Greek yoghurt
- 2 tbsp runny honey* (optional)

- Preheat the grill, oven or George Foreman (where possible, to a medium heat).
- Remove the stalks and the stones from the cherries.
- Mix the cherries, yoghurt and honey in a bowl.
- Slice the almond croissants lengthways. Grill for 2 mins each side, or until warm. Failing a grill, this can be done on a dry frying pan over medium heat.
- Carefully stuff the mix into the croissants.
- Serve with coffee and fruit juice.

*If your honey is too thick, put it semi-submerged in a pot of simmering water for a few minutes to turn it back to liquid.

<u>Mixed Herb Omelette</u>

Have a look online if there are any foraging tours in your area, typically for herbs and/or mushrooms. It's a fun and productive morning in nature. For this dish the herbs were gathered on the banks of the river Elbe. The key is a balance of herbs, whether wild and unfamiliar, or simply a gathering from your window-ledge or greengrocer, or even everyday rocket, parsley and basil.

Ingredients (serves 2):

- 4 large or 5 medium eggs
- 2 tbsp natural yoghurt
- 2 large handfuls of mixed herbs
- 50g strong cheddar
- Rapeseed oil
- Salt, pepper

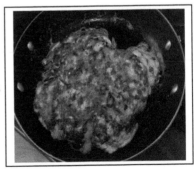

Recipe:

- Heat up a frying pan to a medium heat, add 2 tbsp of oil. Wash and chop the herbs, remove any tough stalks (from say, rosemary). Grate the cheese. Beat the eggs in a bowl with the yoghurt, herbs, cheese and salt and pepper to taste.
- Fry in the pan until cooked on one side (ca. 3 minutes), then carefully (possibly with the aid of a plate) flip over and cook through for another minute or so.
- Serve with bread and some slices of tomato.

Green Beans in Tomato Sauce

Possibly my favourite summer dish. If you don't have fresh redcurrants, redcurrant cordial will work as a substitute. This recipe works perfectly fine with runner beans too. The key is to use the garlic as a proper ingredient here, rather than just a seasoning.

Ingredients (serves 4):

- 600g green beans
- 1 medium onion
- 8 cloves of garlic
- 800g tomatoes
- 100g redcurrants (or 2 tbsp cordial)
- 2 tbsp red wine vinegar
- Olive oil
- 1 red chilli
- Salt, pepper, oregano, tarragon

Recipe:

- Rinse, then top and tail the ends of the green beans. Blanch them whole in a pot of boiling salted water for only 3 minutes. Remove and put to the side.

- Meanwhile, peel and chop the onion as finely as you can, peel and slice the garlic thinly, and chop the chilli finely, removing the stalk and seeds.
- Heat a frying pan to a medium-low heat. Soften the onion, garlic and chilli in 4 tbsp olive oil in this pan for 7-8 minutes. Season with pinches of salt, pepper, oregano and tarragon.
- Chop the tomatoes roughly, removing the core and add to the pan. Add a splash of water, raise the heat to medium and cook through for another 10 minutes.
- Rinse the redcurrants and remove the berries from the stalk. Discard the stalk.
- Add the berries and cook for another 2 minutes, crushing the sauce together with the back of the wooden spoon. If using redcurrant cordial instead, add at this stage. Taste the sauce, it should be a bit sweet.
- Reintroduce the green beans to the pot, along with the vinegar. Cook for another 2 minutes then **taste to check the seasoning and adjust as necessary. The vinegar and the currants should have melded together to create a tangy, sweet-sour balance.**
- Serve warm with a further drizzle of olive oil. This goes great with feta, bread and salad, or alternatively with some cooked grains or buttery pasta.

August

August is the great European shut-down. A mass exodus to the coast leaves cities quieter and reminds us of the social contract offered to us by our states, our reward for commuting through rain, wind and cold. Keycamp holidays first introduced us to the European ideal and new flavours of ice cream, and the first sight of the Mediterranean of the year turns the most embattled, wage-enslaved adults into giddy kids racing into the water. Feet, knees, waist, it's too late you're already in.

The hour of an outdoor aperitif is also well embraceable here, and need not be pretentious nor expensive. I have a lasting memory from a holiday in Menorca sat in the falling dusk with just some olives, salted breadsticks and the coldest can of cerveza to ever be pressed against my cheek.

Summer has its own fatigue and cannot last forever. Cherish the sun on your back, the salty waters of the Mediterranean, the juice of nectarines slurping down your face like sweet teardrops and lock these memories in with the help of summery deep house music. It will keep you sane in January.

- Erobique : Easy
- Energy 52 : Café del Mar
- Three Drives: Greece 2000
- Don Henley : Boys of Summer

August Recipes:

- Peach and Cardamon Chutney
- Sweetcorn and Courgette Fritters
- Fennel, Seaweed and Artichoke Paella
- Cauliflower in Spiced Tomato Sauce

<u>Peach and Cardamom Chutney</u>

Can liven up any sandwich. The same technique works for other fruits, so try playing around with the ingredients, keeping the quantities roughly the same.

Ingredients (makes 3 medium jars):

- 8 medium peaches
- 2 red onions
- 6 cloves garlic
- 2 thumb sized pieces ginger
- 2 red chillis
- 3 heaped tbsp cardamom pods
- 4 tbsp rapeseed oil
- 2 tbsp curry powder
- 1 tbsp turmeric
- 150+g brown sugar
- 100+ml white wine vinegar
- Salt, pepper

Recipe:

- Heat up a pot to a medium heat. Peel and roughly chop the onions. Soften the onion in 4 tbsp of oil with a generous grinding of salt and pepper for 7-8 minutes. **Bear in mind you're seasoning not just the onions, but the added ingredients to come.**
- Peel and thinly slice the garlic, peel and dice the ginger finely, chop the chillis roughly, removing the seeds (unless you want their extra heat).
- Add the chopped garlic, ginger, chilli, the curry powder and the turmeric to the onions and continue cooking for another 2 minutes.
- Cut the peaches into quarters, remove the stone. Remove the seeds from the cardamom shells and add the seeds to the pot. Discard the cardamom shells. Add the peaches, sugar and vinegar to the pot and simmer on a low heat for at least 20 minutes until the consistency is turning somewhat jammy.
- **Taste, checking that it has the right balance of sweet, sour and spice. Add sugar, vinegar or curry powder according to requirements.**
- Keep in mind that the mix should thicken slightly upon cooling.
- When done, allow to cool before storing in sterilised jars.

Sweetcorn and Courgette Fritters

A fried oily bit of goodness that, due to its vegetable content, can't be that bad for you. As there's no garlic or chilli bringing the flavour here, I'd recommend having a good dipping sauce ready. These are class paired with a good quality ketchup.

Ingredients (Serves 4 as a side dish):

- 4 corns on the cob
- 2 medium courgettes
- 100-150g wholemeal flour
- 3 medium eggs
- Vegetable oil
- Salt, pepper

Recipe:

- Rinse, then grate the courgettes directly into a colander. Season generously with salt, then leave to sit for a few minutes.
- **Squeeze as much liquid as possible out of the courgettes, either by using your hands, or by pressing them with the back of a spoon through a sieve. This is necessary for the consistency of the fritters, that they stay dry and stable.** Put the dried courgette into a large bowl.

- Rinse the corn and using a sharp knife, scrape the yellow pieces directly into the same bowl.
- Beat the eggs. Add them to the vegetable mix and stir gently around.
- **Gradually add the flour, spoon by spoon and stir in. You may not need all the flour, you may need more. It depends on the size of the eggs and how little liquid was in the courgettes**. The final mix needs to be on the heavy side of gloopy, but nothing which resembles a bread mix. A texture like greek yoghurt is close to what you're after.
- Heat a wide frying pan up to medium-high. Cover the base of the pan in sunflower oil. Fry small batches (2 spoons worth) of the batter for about 2 mins each side, or until turning brown.
- When cooked, place on a plate lined with kitchen paper.
- Serve with sauce of choice, or some salad and cheese.

*This technique can be adapted for grated carrots, scallions, diced red pepper (fry separately first) etc.

Fennel, Seaweed and Artichoke Paella

The fennel, seaweed and lemon juice complement the taste of the sea, while the artichoke has the texture of cod. The saffron may look out of place in this otherwise relatively cheap collection, but is worth the expenditure. If you have samphire, a bit of that alongside would be excellent.

Ingredients (Serves 4):

- 2 bulbs fennel
- 1 large pepper (red or yellow)
- 1 large tomato
- 4 cloves garlic
- 150 ml white wine, or 75ml pastis
- a handful of seaweed
- 1 can of artichoke hearts (ca. 250g drained weight)
- 100g frozen peas
- 350-400g paella rice (if not, risotto rice is fine)
- Seasoning: 1 heaped tbsp Spanish paprika, a few threads of saffron, fresh parsley, salt, pepper
- 2 lemons
- Olive oil
- 2 vegetable stock cubes

Recipe:

- To prepare the fennel, chop the sticks off the top. Slice in half vertically, then slice both halves again vertically. From there, at an angle remove the tough inner core and discard the core. Wash the remaining fennel as dirt can get underneath their layers.
- Cut fennel into thinnish slices, like you would with onions for a stir fry. Cut the pepper into 1cm cubes. Peel and slice the garlic into batons. Chop the tomato roughly, removing the core. In a generous amount of olive oil (start with 4 tbsp and add more as needed) in your biggest frying pan (you'll probably need to use 2 frying pans), soften the fennel, peppers, garlic and tomato on a medium-low heat for 10 mins. This can be accelerated if the pan can be covered.
- Season with paprika and black pepper. Stir around and add another glug of olive oil if the pan is too dry.
- Soak the saffron strands in a small quantity of boiling water. Prepare the veg stock with boiling water according to package instructions. Soak the seaweed in cold water to desalt it (10 mins) (If using dried seaweed, follow packet instruction and soak in hot water).
- Add the rice to the pan and coat it in the now reddish oil. Turn the heat up to medium and toss it around the pan. Add the wine or pastis and leave for 30 seconds as it bubbles, or until you can no longer smell the raw alcohol off it.

- Add the saffron along with its soaking water. Add enough vegetable stock to cover the rice by 2cm (you may need to add more later).
- Chop the seaweed and add to the pan. Stir the rice around gently, then flatten it to even it out. Simmer without stirring it further.
- If the water level drops below the top of the rice, then top up with some hot vegetable stock. The rice should take 20 mins to cook.
- 5 mins before the end, soak the frozen peas in boiling water for 30 seconds. Add to the pan.
- Drain the artichoke hearts, cut the artichokes in half and add to pan.
- Check if any more stock is needed.
- Squeeze the juice of one lemon directly into the pan. **Squeeze the juice through your fingers as a natural filter for any pips.**
- Add some more black pepper and a glug of olive oil. Taste and add salt if necessary. When the rice is cooked, turn the heat off, cover with a plate and leave to sit for at least 5 mins.
- Chop the other lemon into quarters to serve with the dish. Serve with a simple salad and bask in the compliments.
- Store any leftovers in the fridge.

Cauliflower in Spiced Tomato Sauce

Try source your cauliflower from a proper greengrocer's or farmer's market for this one, it really makes a difference. Serve either with some grains, or with flatbread and salad. Quantities can easily be doubled.

Ingredients (serves 4 as a side dish):

- Half a head of cauliflower
- 1 onion
- 4 cloves garlic
- 1 thumb sized piece ginger
- 1 red chilli
- 6 tbsp olive oil
- 2 tbsp ras el hanout
- 8 medium tomatoes
- 2 tbsp tomato purée
- 1 handful of almonds
- 1 tbsp turmeric
- Squeeze of lemon juice
- 4 tbsp chopped fresh coriander
- Salt, pepper

Recipe:
- Wash the cauliflower and break off the florets as they naturally fall. Any remaining stalk can be chopped into 1cm cubes. You can use the leaves too, just remove the thick stem in the middle.

- Heat 4tbsp oil in a frying pan on a medium-high heat, then fry the cauliflower until it begins to brown (should take 6 or 7 mins). Continue cooking for another 2 minutes. Season with a pinch of salt. Remove the cauliflower and drop the heat to low.
- Peel and finely chop the onion. Soften the onion in the same pan with a touch of salt and pepper for 7-8 minutes. Add another tbsp or 2 of olive oil if it's too dry.
- Peel and slice the garlic finely, peel and chop the ginger finely, chop the chilli into thin strips. Add the garlic, ginger, chilli, ras el hanout and turmeric and cook for another minute.
- Chop the tomatoes roughly, removing the core. Add the tomatoes to the pan. Increase the heat and cook through for another 5 minutes, add the tomato purée and cook for another minute.
- Return the cauliflower to the pan, along with the almonds, chopped coriander and lemon juice. Add a splash of water if it's not 'saucy' enough.
- Continue cooking on a low heat for another couple of minutes, then check the seasoning and add whatever you may feel is missing. Allow to cool slightly before serving.

September

La Rentrée. Hopefully refreshed and with a renewed enthusiasm, we return to our desks, shops and factories. September shares the sense of new beginnings that January traditionally dominates. It's time for new projects to kick off, and any changes to be embraced with open arms.

The first chill in the air is also to be embraced. With a creeping evening darkness and a jacket accompanying us on our journeys, it is clear that change is afoot. The return to normality is a necessary part of life's cycle, one which we should equally appreciate, for it is the nature of contrast and the contrast in nature which livens up our world, and of course our dinner plates.

Take the time to go for a walk in the woods for a breath of fresh cool air. The colours of autumn show themselves in the trees; tomato red, pumpkin orange and spinach green flutter gently onto the walnut brown forest pathways. If you prefer to spend your evenings in the warmth of your local, European soccer is back in full swing. Mark a Sampdoria v Palermo fixture with Pesto Genovese v Caponata for your evening meals.

- Manic Street Preachers : Autumn Song
- Chicane : Autumn Tactics
- Smashing Pumpkins : 1979
- Seeed : Ticket

September Recipes:
- Aubergine, Tomato, Mozzarella Bake
- Broccoli Orzo and Buttery Chard, with Tomato Salsa
- Tofush and Chips
- Apple Cake

Aubergine, Tomato and Mozzarella Bake

An ideal dish to present to guests. Be sure to secure a final portion for yourself to eat in a decadent sandwich the next day. Serve with salad, bread and a heap of red wine.

Ingredients (serves 4-6):

- 4 medium aubergines
- 3 packets of mozzarella (125g drained weight each)
- 6-8 lasagne sheets

For the sauce:
- 1 red onion
- 2 cans chopped tomatoes
- 3 tbsp tomato purée
- 2 red chillis
- 4 cloves garlic
- 1 tbsp dried oregano and/or thyme
- 1 tbsp vinegar
- Olive oil
- Salt, pepper

Recipe:

- Preheat an oven to 200c. Top and tail the aubergines. Slice them relatively thinly (1/2 a cm), toss in a bowl with 4tbsp olive oil and a generous grinding of salt and pepper.
- Put the aubergines onto a roasting dish (same deep one you'll use for the bake) and put into the oven for about 20 mins until cooked through.
- Meanwhile, prepare the tomato sauce. Peel and finely chop the onion and garlic, chop the chilli into thin rings.
- Heat 2tbsp olive oil in a pot to a medium-low heat. Soften the onion, garlic, chilli and dried herbs with a pinch of salt and pepper in the pot for 10 minutes.
- Add the cans of chopped tomatoes, the tomato purée and 1 tbsp of vinegar. Rinse the remainder of the tomato cans out with a splash of water and add that in too. Simmer for another 10 minutes. Turn off the heat.
- When the aubergines are done, prepare the dish in alternate layers: aubergine, tomato sauce, mozzarella. For the lasagne sheets, break them up and **scatter them through the dish, tucked in within the sauce so they'll get properly cooked. You may want to add a short pouring of hot water over the top of the final dish to ensure they're covered and will cook well.** Finish with a final layer of cheese.

- Bake in the 200c oven for 30 minutes until structurally set together, checking halfway. Remove from oven and allow to cool for at least 10 minutes before serving.

Broccoli Orzo and Buttery Chard, with Tomato Salsa

Orzo is a delightful rice-shaped pasta. Try it here loaded with green veg. You can use a mix of tenderstem and regular broccoli. For extra flavour, add parmesan to the chard.

Ingredients (serves 2):

- 150g orzo
- 300g broccoli
- 150g rainbow chard
- 2 cloves garlic
- 100g feta
- 3 tbsp olive oil
- 3 tbsp butter
- 3 slices of lemon
- 2 bay leaves
- Salt, pepper, chilli flakes, oregano

Salsa:
- 12 cherry tomatoes
- 1 large tomato
- 1 tbsp balsamic vinegar
- 2 tbsp olive oil
- 2 cloves garlic
- Salt, pepper

Recipe:

- Firstly, prepare the chard. Wash it thoroughly, then tear the stalks and the leaves into 2 separate bowls.
- Peel and thinly slice 2 cloves of garlic.
- Heat 3 tbsp olive oil in a small pot on a medium heat. Cook the garlic and chard stalks for 4 minutes. Season with salt, pepper, oregano and chilli flakes.
- Add the leaves and leave to wilt for another 4 minutes. Stir in the butter. Turn off the heat.
- Meanwhile, for the orzo, begin to cook it in boiling salted water as you would pasta. Add the bay leaves and lemon slices.
- Wash and chop the broccoli into bitesize pieces. The stalk can be peeled and chopped into 1cm cubes.

- After 5 minutes of the orzo cooking, add the broccoli and continue cooking for another 7 minutes. **Increase the heat as you add the broccoli as the water's temperature will drop otherwise.**
- Prepare the salsa. Peel and finely chop the garlic, add to a bowl with salt, pepper and vinegar and leave sit for 2 minutes. Chop the tomatoes roughly into different shapes, then add to the bowl along with the olive oil.
- Once ready, drain the orzo/broccoli pot. Cube the feta and stir it in.
- Serve the orzo on plates with the chard spooned over, and tomato salsa on the side.

Tofush and Chips

Friday night chippy tea if you live in Prestwich. Feel free to make extra tofush for the next night's dinner. Serve this with either salad or mushy peas. If you can get some samphire, that would also be an excellent accompaniment.

Ingredients (serves 4):

Tofush:
- 400g firm tofu
- 4 tbsp dried seaweed
- 1 bottle of beer
- 150g flour
- 1 tsp baking powder
- Salt and pepper
- Sunflower oil
- 2 lemons, to serve

Chips:
- 6 large potatoes
- Salt and pepper
- Sunflower oil

Recipe:

- Firstly make the batter*. Put the flour and baking powder in a large bowl and season with and grind of salt and pepper. Make a well in the centre and gradually pour in some beer (likely 150-200ml) and stir until it has a consistency similar to natural yoghurt.
- Drink the rest of the beer. Leave the batter to rest in the fridge for 30 minutes.
- Begin the chips. Preheat the oven to 220c. Wash the potatoes and slice into chips. No need to peel. Put onto an oven dish, season with salt and pepper and add 4tbsp of oil, then toss the chips around.
- Roast in the oven for 30-40 minutes, tossing again halfway through.
- Meanwhile, put the dried seaweed in a bowl and pour over boiling water to rest for a few minutes, or according to packet instructions. Drain when done.
- Remove the tofu from the packaging. Cut the tofu into lengths. Aim for 8 strips.
- Put a few sheets of kitchen paper** on a chopping board. Put the tofu slices on top, then cover with another few sheets of kitchen paper. Put a weight (e.g. a plate with a few tins on it) on top, so as to press excess moisture out of the tofu. Leave to rest for 10 minutes.

- When ready, wrap the seaweed around the tofu slices, or press onto them, however you can get them to stay together.
- Heat about 6 tbsp sunflower oil in a frying pan to a high heat. The base of the pan should be covered lightly with the oil, so add more or less as you see fit. Dip the tofu and seaweed into the batter, **then fry until the batter is cooked solid on one side – gently tossing the pan will see the pieces move in unison.** Turn the tofu slices over, cook till the batter is golden on the other side, then remove onto a plate lined with kitchen paper.* This should take 1 ½ to 2 minutes per side.
- Check the chips and remove from the oven.
- Serve the tofush and chips along with the accompaniments of your choice.

*Any leftover batter can be used to coat vegetables and fry them while the oil is still hot. Courgette and aubergine are particularly suited to this.

**This step isn't always necessary, depends on the firmness of the tofu you've bought. Avoid silken tofu at all costs for this recipe.

Apple Cake

A simple batter, not overly sweet, which follows my principle that the best desserts are those which can be eaten for breakfast. Loosely baked on an old pal Hania's cake, which originally used rose jam instead of apple purée.

Ingredients (serves 6-8):

- 300g flour
- 250g butter
- 150g sugar + 2 tbsp extra
- 4 large apples
- 3 eggs
- 2 handfuls müsli
- 2 handfuls mixed seeds
- 1 tsp baking powder
- 1 tsp cinnamon
- A small pinch of salt

Recipe:

- Preheat the oven to 190c.
- Wash and chop the apples roughly (peeling isn't necessary) and put in a pot to cook on medium heat with 1tbsp sugar and a splash of water. After 5 minutes it should be close to mashable. If not, add a splash of water and continue another few mins until so. Add a teaspoon of cinnamon and stir in.
- Cube the butter into about 1cm pieces. In a large bowl, mix together the flour, butter and sugar. Beat in the eggs, add the müsli, mixed seeds, baking powder, and salt. Stir together.
- Line a long bread tin (ca. 8x8x25cm) with greaseproof paper. Pour 2/3 of the cake batter out, smoothen it, then pour all the apple mix on top and smoothen it out. To conclude, dot the remainder of the batter over the cake, covering as much of the apple mix as you can manage.
- Sprinkle 1 tbsp sugar over the cake and bake in the oven for 30-40 minutes, or until cooked through (check with a skewer).
- Allow to cool slightly before serving with a dollop of yoghurt and a coffee.

October

Autumn intensifies itself. The weekly routine becomes more familiar; work, work, sports in the evening, work, work, nip out for a drink, work, then start the weekend with a potter around the shops and the weekly spontaneous stop-off into the café and bookies. All seems to be going to plan until Udinese concede a last minute equaliser.

The rain seems more frequent. You put on a scarf for the first time since before summer. It's probably either some checked tartan-y design or of a fallen giant soccer team. Newcastle, Feyenoord and St. Étienne themselves feel like the latter stretches of autumn. Past glories look very unlikely to be repeated anytime soon, and the grey everyday of the wealthy's dominance in their domestic scenes looks to continue uninterrupted.

With the change from the bright season to the dark one, this can be a very reflective time of year. Once you get deep enough into your routine, it's probably the first time where you will pause, look back, and say to yourself "Fuck, that was a class summer!". Mediterranean sunsets can seem a very long way off when the darkness is strangling the life out of your evenings. The markets are still full and bustling, so recreate your happiest holiday memories on the dinner plate.

- Ash : Walking Barefoot
- Martha : Ice Cream and Sunscreen
- Everything But The Girl : Lullaby of Clubland
- Sharon Van Etten : 17

October Recipes:
- Courgette Tagliatelle
- Potato Soup
- Mushrooms on Toast
- Gnocchi in Cheese Sauce with Kale Salad

Courgette Tagliatelle

A faux pasta dish. If you wanna eat this with cooked tagliatelle, you don't have to wait for my approval. Works well as a side dish, or as a main with any kind of 'fillet' fried and placed on top.

Ingredients (serves 2):

- 2 large courgettes
- 1 red chilli
- 4 cloves garlic
- 1 lemon
- 6 tbsp olive oil
- Oregano, salt, pepper
- 4 tbsp mixed seeds
- Parmesan (optional)

Recipe:

- Rinse the courgettes, then top and tail them. With the side of a box grater, grate the courgettes into long ribbons. Don't worry if you get a lot of short ones.
- Peel and chop the garlic into thin slices, chop the chilli into thin strips, removing the seeds.

- Heat 2tbsp of olive oil in a large pot to a low heat. Soften the garlic and chilli in the pot for 2 minutes, until turning fragrant. Add the oregano, salt and pepper and continue cooking for another 30 seconds.
- Add the rest of the olive oil. Grate the zest of the lemon directly into the pot. Squeeze the lemon juice in too.
- Then, add the same quantity water as is currently in the pot (i.e. the juice and oil, should be about 8-10 tbsp), and bring the heat up to medium-high.
- Add the courgettes and **stir them around the pot vigorously and continuously for about 5 minutes, until they are all well covered in the cooking liquor and have softened a bit.**
- Sprinkle the mixed seeds in, and add parmesan if using.

Potato Soup

Warming, hearty soup, ideal to slurp out of a bowl while sat on the couch. Thyme or rosemary can be used instead of the marjoram.

Ingredients (serves 4):

- 1 large red onion
- 2 medium carrots
- 1 stick of celery
- 4 medium potatoes
- 4 cloves of garlic
- 4tbsp thyme or marjoram
- Salt, pepper
- 3 tbsp mustard seeds (optional)
- 100g soup mix*
- 1 litre vegetable stock
- 4 tbsp rapeseed oil + extra to drizzle
- Mature cheddar to grate on top (optional)

Recipe:

- Either at the start of the day, or the night before, put the soup mix in a bowl of water and cover.
- Peel and chop the onion and garlic finely. Chop the carrot and celery into ½ cm cubes. Heat 4 tbsp of rapeseed oil in a

pot to a medium-low heat. Soften the onion, garlic, carrot and celery in the pot with a pinch of salt, cooking for about 10 minutes, being conscious to not let the onion and garlic burn.

- Season generously with pepper and add the mustard seeds. Add the thyme or marjoram. Continue cooking softly.
- Meanwhile, peel the potatoes and **chop them roughly. They should be about 2cm in diameter, as you want them to maintain some of their structure in the soup.**
- Rinse the soup mix and add to the pot.
- Pour over the vegetable stock, bring to the boil, then simmer gently for about 20 mins (or according to the cooking time of the package soup mix).
- Add the potato cubes for a further 10 minutes and continue cooking.
- Check everything's cooked through and seasoned correctly.
- Serve hot in a bowl with the cheese if using, a drizzle of rapeseed oil and some bread and butter on the side.

*soup mix is a mix of dried pearl barley and pulses. Could be replaced here with some red lentils and broken pasta pieces. In which case, don't bother to soak it beforehand.

Mushrooms on Toast

A selfish lunch for one using not the cheapest oyster mushrooms. Other wild mushrooms could be substituted here. Serve with a simple green salad.

Ingredients (serves 1):

- 4 large oyster mushrooms
- 2 cloves of garlic
- 2 tbsp rapeseed oil
- Salt and pepper
- 2 tbsp fresh parsley
- 1 tbsp lemon juice
- 1-2 tbsp of butter
- 1 tbsp capers
- 2 slices of bread

Recipe:

- Delicately rinse any dirt off the mushrooms, then pat dry with a paper towel. Slice thickly into lengths.
- Heat the oil to medium high in a pan, add the mushrooms and stir fry for 3 or 4 minutes until beginning to brown. **The slices should resemble leftover roast chicken being fried in a pan.**

- Peel and thinly slice the garlic. Add to the pan and cook for another minute. Lower the heat, then add the parsley, butter, capers and lemon juice, season with salt and pepper and switch the heat off, while continuing to stir.
- Toast the bread. Butter when ready (optional, some may find this a bit too greasy).
- Spoon the mix onto the bread, and enjoy.

Gnocchi in Cheese Sauce with Kale Salad

The crisp, freshness of the kale adds a healthy balance to the decadence of the cheese sauce. Goes very well with some grilled vegetables and/or a beetroot salad. A happy reconstruction of one of my favourite meals ever had, in a konoba in Split, with friends old and new.

Ingredients (serves 4):

Gnocchi in Sauce:
- 800g gnocchi
- 2 tbsp olive oil
- 3 tbsp butter
- 2 tbsp flour
- 400-500ml milk
- 100-150g cheese of choice
- Salt, pepper
- Nutmeg, a short grating

Kale Salad:
- 1 medium head of kale (ca. 200g)
- 4 medium carrots
- 12 sundried tomatoes in oil
- 2 handfuls of walnuts (or other nuts)
- 1 tbsp mustard
- 1 tbsp cider vinegar
- 1 tbsp honey
- 3 tbsp olive oil
- Salt and pepper

Recipe:

- For the salad, remove the leaves off the kale stalks, tear the leaves up roughly, put them in a colander and wash thoroughly. In a large bowl, mix together the oil, honey, mustard and vinegar along with a splash of water and grind in enough salt and pepper.
- Add the kale into the bowl. Grate the carrots in directly. Slice the sundried tomatoes into thick strips and add them in, along with the nuts, then mix together thoroughly with your hands.
- Heat the milk up either in the microwave or in a small pot.
- For the sauce, **make a béchamel; heat 2tbsp oil and 3tbsp butter together in another pot over medium heat. Add in the flour and let cook gently for 30-60 seconds. Add in ¼ of the hot milk, then stir and allow to cook. The mix shouldn't be turning brown, but should start yellow and gradually become whiter. Once thickened, add some more milk and stir again**, and continue with the rest of it. You may not need all the milk.
- **If you feel the sauce is too thick, bear in mind that some pasta cooking water can be used to thin it out. If it's too thin, remember that the cheese will help thicken it.**
- Add in your cheese of choice, either cubed or grated. Be conscious of the cheese's strength and possible saltiness. Gorgonzola, for example, would need a lower amount than,

say, emmental. Season afterwards with some salt and pepper, and grate in some fresh nutmeg. Stir the nutmeg in and you should be able to lightly smell the nutmeg's influence within the mix.

- For the gnocchi, cook according to packet instructions.
- Once cooked, add the gnocchi to the sauce, along with a splash of pasta cooking water. Stir together to combine. Serve in bowls with the kale salad and other accompaniments.

*Note: The Kale Salad works very well on its own in a lunchbox if you add in some cooked grains and some feta or cheddar.

November

It's little consolation to say that we're still in the omnishaded autumn when your feet are freezing because you underestimated the icy concrete and you've holes in the bottom of your socks, which you keep meaning to throw out but somehow after every wash you say they'll do for another week.

November can hurt. The darkness comes out of nowhere, and you start leaving work in bleak emptiness, with the rainy mist hanging above you to full cinematic effect. It's the first test winter brings us. Yes, I know it's autumn still. However lifeless November may feel, it is nonetheless our banal. A Tuesday in a November is an appropriate litmus test of your satisfaction with your current situation.

Take the time to get out for walks at lunchtime or on weekend mornings. Your sanity will thank you for granting them some daylight. Enjoy ordinary existence before the premature decorations come up, such as a secularly illuminated city centre on the way home from work without a mechanically waving white-bearded man in red.

I find November's a great month for nights out. A Saturday night in town also carries the current vibes of a city's population, and there's a pleasure in being surrounded by people determined to escape the darkness of their everyday routine. A few more fun and energetic tracks to counter the subdued atmosphere and get you dancing in the kitchen.

- Sons of Southern Ulster : Pop Inn
- The Housemartins : I Smell Winter
- The Go Team : Buy Nothing Day
- Tilly and The Wall : Beat Control

November Recipes:
- Leek, Goat's Cheese and Thyme Risotto
- Lemon and Garlic Potatoes
- Quick Courgette Quiche
- Kale, Gorgonzola and Walnut Pasta

Leek, Goat's Cheese and Thyme Risotto

Creamy without cream, reassuring without doubt. Leeks react well to steaming or boiling, so avoid the temptation to fry them in the same pot.

Ingredients (serves 4):

- 1 large onion
- 2 large leeks
- 1 medium carrot
- 1 stick of celery
- 1 red chilli (optional)
- 4 cloves garlic
- 4 tbsp olive oil
- 350-400g risotto rice
- 2 vegetable stock cubes (to make 1 litre stock)
- 100ml white wine
- 200g goat's cheese (a typical supermarket roll of chèvre is fine here)
- 4 tbsp butter
- A handful fresh thyme sprigs
- A handful of walnuts or pumpkin seeds
- Salt, pepper
- Parmesan (optional)

Recipe:

- Peel and finely chop the onion and garlic, finely chop the chilli if using, dice the carrot and the celery into ½ cm cubes each. Heat the olive oil in a large pot to a medium-low heat, then soften the above chopped vegetables for 10 minutes. Add a few grinds of salt to help the process along.
- After about 10 minutes when the onions are more translucent, bring the heat up to medium-high, add 2 tbsp of butter and all the rice and let it toast while stirring around for 30 seconds.
- Prepare the veg stock with powder and boiling water. The stock should be kept hot throughout, so it doesn't slow the cooking process. If using fresh stock, heat it up in another pot.
- **Add the wine and mix around for another minute until almost evaporated, the raw alcohol smell will eventually soften down.**
- Rinse the thyme sprigs. Drop the heat to medium-low, add the thyme.
- Gradually add some stock every few minutes (or as the mix starts to dry out) and stir gently. The aim is that there is always just enough hot stock covering the rice. Continue to do so until the rice is cooked. This should take 18-20 mins.
- Meanwhile, prepare the leeks. Bring a pot of water to the boil, add salt. Top and tail the leeks. Cut them in half

lengthways, and then rinse thoroughly to get rid of any hidden dirt inside. Chop them into rough bitesize chunks, drop the heat to medium-low and simmer for 5 minutes.

- As the risotto approaches doneness, check the texture and continue cooking another few minutes if needs be. Cut the goat's cheese into cubes and add in. Grate the lemon zest in, then squeeze its juice in to accompany it. Add the remaining butter, stir in the cooked leeks, then cover, switch the heat off and leave to rest for 5 minutes.
- Serve in bowls with some side salad and the nuts/seeds sprinkled on top.

Lemon and Garlic Potatoes

Delightful as a side dish to a fillet of something, or even as the centrepiece itself, served with some fried greens.

Ingredients (serves 2):

- 600g potatoes
- 6 cloves garlic
- 1 red chilli
- 4+ tbsp olive oil
- 1 lemon
- 4 tbsp mixed seeds
- Salt, pepper

Recipe:

- Wash the potatoes thoroughly, scrubbing off any dirt. Slice them very thinly lengthwise (less than ½ a cm thick), then rinse again.
- Boil some water in the kettle. Peel and slice the garlic into thin strips. Deseed and chop the chilli finely.
- Heat 4tbsp olive oil in a frying pan to a high heat, then add the potato slices, trying to cover all with the oil as you toss them around. You may need to do this in 2 batches. In which case, cook half the potatoes, remove, then cook the

other half, adding the garlic and chilli, before returning the rest of the potatoes to the pan.

- Once the potatoes begin to turn brown, turn the heat down to medium. Add the garlic and chilli and continue to toss around for 3-4 minutes. If the pan is too dry, add an extra tbsp of olive oil
- Drop the heat to low. Add a splash of boiling water. Grate the zest of the lemon directly into the pan. Squeeze the juice of the lemon directly in too, then stir around and cover with a plate. The idea is that a light layer of liquid on the bottom is steaming the mix.
- According to taste, you may add more oil or seasonings here. **The potatoes should be oily, but not swimming in oil.** When the potatoes are cooked through, add the seeds and divide onto 2 plates with your side serving of choice.

Quick Courgette Quiche

This looks impressive with minimal effort. The oven dish used was 23x23x8cm, and served 4. For a bigger dish, increase the quantities accordingly.

Ingredients (serves 4):

- A 375g sheet of shortcrust pastry
- 2 medium courgettes
- 5 large eggs
- 6 tbsp natural yoghurt
- 150g grated gouda
- 3 tbsp smooth mustard
- Salt, pepper

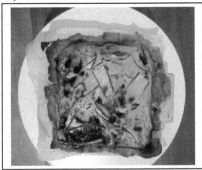

Recipe:

- Preheat the oven to 200c. Wash the courgettes, trim the ends off and slice thinly lengthwise, using a mandolin. Don't worry if it doesn't come out neatly. Set aside.
- Roll the pastry out into the oven dish, using the paper sheet given in the packet as a lining for the dish. **If there's too much pastry in the packet you bought, cut the ends off which you won't use and save for another recipe (for**

example, roll flat and top with chopped tomatoes and cheese like a mini pizza).

- In a large bowl, beat the eggs with the yoghurt and mustard. Add the courgettes. Season with salt and pepper and add the grated gouda (substitutions here also possible). If it's too thick, add a bit more milk and/or yoghurt.
- Pour the mix into the pastry-lined dish and even out the surfaces with a fork or spoon. Using a pastry brush, brush the external pastry with some extra milk (massage milk in with your fingers if you don't have a pastry brush).
- Bake in the oven at 200c for 30 minutes, or until cooked through and a knife comes out clean.
- Allow to cool slightly for at least 5 minutes before cutting into portions.
- Serve with a bulky salad and some bread. Or serve with baked beans. Depends on your mood.

Kale, Gorgonzola and Walnut Pasta

You say gorgon-zola, I think of Gianfranco. I picture a homesick Sardinian in 1990s London not being able to get the same winter greens as at home, and substituting Stilton into this recipe, which you are also entitled to do.

Ingredients (serves 4):

- 400g pasta (short types are best here)
- 1 head kale
- 150-200g gorgonzola
- A large handful of shelled walnuts
- 4 cloves garlic
- 1 red chilli
- 6 tbsp olive oil
- 1 lemon
- Salt, pepper

Recipe:

- Remove the leaves from the stalks of the kale. Break the leaves up into small pieces and put in a colander. Discard the stalks into the compost bin.
- Peel and thinly slice the garlic, and slice the chilli into small rounds. Heat the olive oil in a pan on a low heat and add

the garlic and chilli, along with a generous amount of pepper and a small bit of salt (the cheese will add some saltiness to the overall dish).

- Boil enough water in a pot, add salt and cook the pasta to packet instructions.
- Rinse the kale thoroughly then add to the frying pan and increase the heat to medium. Cook for about 5 minutes, stirring frequently.
- Zest the lemon directly into the pan, then cut it in half and squeeze its juice into it. Cube the gorgonzola roughly and add it into the pan. Try 150g first, before later deciding if you want more.
- Add the walnuts along with a splash of pasta cooking water and stir to create a creamy sauce.
- Drain the pasta once cooked, reserving a bit more cooking water.
- Mix the pasta into the sauce along with another splash of cooking water.
- Taste the pasta and add more cheese, salt or pepper as necessary.
- Serve in bowls with some slices of raw veg (e.g. radishes, carrots) alongside and eat it all with a spoon, curled up on the couch watching a highlights reel of Gianfranco's best goals.

December

The weather seems to play less of a role in December. Yes, it's cold, but we seem to tolerate it better. Cold isn't the worst thing when you're on your way to somewhere warm. In the medium term that may be the Mediterranean next summer, but here we're just happy to get home, to a friend's, or to the pub.

Healthy eating can be difficult in this month. Sugar abounds, and boxes of cheap branded confectionary do the rounds in the workplace and as less-than-desired presents. If you're getting somebody something vaguely thoughtful, make it something they'll want to consume in January: good quality tea, coffee, olive oil, fancy storecupboard items. When common practice is overconsumption, take a step back and look after your physical well-being.

Christmas is a great excuse to contact old friends. Drop them a message, and even if you can't physically meet up, that candle stays lit until the opportunity presents itself. Don't over burden yourself for a veggie centrepiece at dinner either. The people you're sharing these moments with would rather your company and attention with a ready made veggie dish than you spending hours cracking walnuts to stuff in a savoury pie. Enjoy the human contact, sit around with some snacks and drinks, and nostalgise about how Christmas Number Ones in the 80s were actually decent tunes.

- Smith and Burrows : This Ain't New Jersey
- Kate Bush : December Will Be Magic Again
- Aidan Moffat and RM Hubbert : A Ghost Story for Christmas
- St. Étienne : I Was Born on Christmas Day

December Recipes:
- Mushroom and Lentil Ragù with Polenta
- Vegetable Crisps
- Pumpkin Soup
- Pasta with Chickpeas and Brown Bread

Mushroom and Lentil Ragù with Polenta

Lentils are eaten across Europe on New Year's Eve and are said to bring fortune. This is an impressive and uncomplicated way to feed a crowd, and the quantities can be increased as needed. Delightful with some veggie sausages.

Ingredients (serves 6):

Ragù:
- 1 large onion
- 1 leek
- 1 carrot
- 1 stick of celery
- 1 yellow pepper
- 400g mushrooms
- 2 x 400g cans of brown lentils
- 2 x 400g can of chopped tomatoes
- 100ml red wine
- 1 heaped tbsp smoked paprika
- 1 tbsp dried tarragon
- 6 cloves garlic
- 6+ tbsp rapeseed oil
- 3 tbsp tomato purée
- 2 tbsp gravy granules
- Salt, pepper

Polenta:
- 500g polenta
- 500ml boiling water
- 500ml milk
- 150g assorted cheeses (could use the ends of a cheeseboard. If using stronger cheeses exclusively reduce to 100g)
- 1 veg stock cube
- 4 tbsp rapeseed oil
- 2+ tbsp butter
- Pepper

Recipe:

- Peel and finely chop the onion and garlic. Top and tail the leek, cut in half lengthways and rinse thoroughly before chopping into 1cm semi-rings. Roughly chop the carrot, celery and pepper, discarding its stem and seeds.
- In a large pot on a medium-low heat, soften the above vegetables in 6 tbsp rapeseed oil with a generous pinch of salt for 10-15 minutes.
- Wash, roughly chop and add the mushrooms. Cook for another 5-10 minutes, until the mushrooms look and smell cooked.
- Add the paprika, tarragon and a generous grinding of black pepper and mix in, add another glug of oil in if it seems too dry. Continue to cook for one minute.

- Add the wine and increase the heat to medium-high so it bubbles off until you can no longer smell raw alcohol (about 1 minute).
- Drain the cans of lentils, add them. Add in the cans of tomatoes, and rinse the end out with a splash of water and add in. Add the gravy granules and tomato purée, along with a splash of hot water. Bring to the beginning of a boil then drop the heat to low and let simmer for 10-15 minutes. **Add more water at any point if necessary, but this should be fairly thick, rather than a liquidy sauce.**
- Meanwhile, prepare the polenta. Heat the oil and 2 tbsp of butter in a pot. Heat the milk up either in a microwave or in a separate pot.
- Add ¾ of the polenta, and then half the hot water and milk, along with the crumbled veg stock cube and some ground pepper. Stir together. Cook over a low heat and stir it gently as it thickens out.
- Check the quantities in case there's already enough for your guests. If not, add the remaining ¼ of the polenta along with some water and milk.
- Continue to stir over the low heat for 10 minutes, adding hot milk and water as necessary.
- Chop the cheese into small pieces and add to the polenta. Stir for another minute, then taste and check seasoning, and if it needs any more butter or oil. Once done, remove from the heat.

- Taste the ragù, and season further as desired.
- Serve the two beside each other in bowls.

*Note: Leftover ragù is a fine pasta sauce.

*Leftover polenta can be flattened out onto a plate while still warm, and the next day sliced into fry-able portions. Would be a handy lunch with either a mixed salad or some beans.

<u>Vegetable Crisps</u>

Easier than you think and delectable with some booze. Add herbs or spices as you see fit, or try with other root veg (celeriac, turnip, beetroot).

Ingredients (makes 2 medium bowls per veg):

- 1 medium head kale (or 200g)
- 2 large parsnips
- 2 large carrots
- 4 tbsp rapeseed oil
  per roasting tray
- Salt, pepper

Recipe:

- Preheat the oven to 180c.
- Rinse all veg thoroughly.
- Kale – remove the leaves from the stalks. Discard the stalks. Tear the leaves roughly.
- Carrots – cut the bottom end off the carrots, then grate finely in long strips on a mandolin. Discard the top end.
- Parsnips - cut the bottom end off the parsnips, then grate finely in long strips on a mandolin. If the parsnips are too tough, just slice them as thinly as possible. Discard the top end.
- All veg, done separately - massage with 4tbsp oil, some salt and pepper. **Start conservatively with the oil, as you may not want to use all of it. You just want a light coating of oil and seasoning over the vegetables.**
- Put on 3 separate roasting trays and roast for 25-30 minutes, or until the corners start to char. It's probably better to roast these separately, as a crowded oven will be ineffective.
- Serve with hummus, guacamole or similar dips.

Smashing Pumpkin Soup

In season through most of autumn and winter, this soup is velvety and soothing. The pumpkin can be replaced here by butternut squash or sweet potato. If you want to bulk this out, you can add red lentils to the soup, or add a couple of tomatoes and/or peppers with the roasting pumpkin.

Ingredients (serves 4, with sandwiches):

- 1 medium pumpkin
- 1 red onion
- 1 stick celery
- 1 small carrot
- 4 cloves garlic
- 1 veg stock cube
- 4 tbsp rapeseed oil
- Salt, pepper
- 4 tbsp pumpkin seed oil (optional)
- 4 tbsp pumpkin seeds (optional)

Recipe:

- Preheat oven to 220c.
- Wash the pumpkin and remove the top and bottom from it. Cut it in half and scoop out the seeds.

- Cut the halves into 1cm thick strips.
- **Don't bother peeling the pumpkin, the skin is fine to eat when cooked. Just remove any unappetising looking grey bits from the skin.**
- Lightly crush the garlic cloves with the side of a knife, then toss them in whole with the pumpkin into a roasting dish. Season with salt and pepper, add 2 tbsp rapeseed oil, then roast until cooked through (15-20 mins).
- Meanwhile, peel and finely dice the onion. Cook it on a low heat in a pot, with 2 tbsp rapeseed oil and a touch of salt for 8 minutes.
- Roughly chop the carrots and celery. Add them to the pot and continue the low cooking for another 5 minutes.
- Heat the vegetable stock if using fresh, or simply mix powder with boiling water.
- Once the pumpkin is ready, remove the skins from the garlic cloves. Add the garlic, pumpkin and vegetable stock to the pot, and simmer all together for 2 minutes.
- Blend. Check the seasoning and adjust as necessary.
- Serve in bowls with a sprinkling of pumpkin seeds and a drizzle of pumpkin seed oil. Goes great with a toasted cheese sandwich.

Pasta with Chickpeas and Brown Bread

A versatile supper popularised by rooting through Mona and Aidan's store cupboard. Soda bread is suggested, but can be swapped for your own national loaf.

Ingredients (serves 4):

- 400g pasta
- 2 cans of chickpeas
- 3 slices of soda bread (40-50g)
- 1 lemon
- 100g strong white cheddar
- 4 cloves garlic
- 1 red chilli
- 4 tbsp olive oil, plus extra to serve
- 200g spinach or 120g rocket
- 2 tbsp butter (optional)
- Salt, pepper

Recipe:

- Cook pasta according to packet instructions in salted boiling water.
- Cut the bread into 1cm cubes. In a frying pan, heat 3 tbsp of the oil to high and add the bread cubes. Stir fry until

turning golden brown, textured like sun, then remove from the pan and put on a plate.

- Peel and thinly slice the garlic, chop the chilli finely. Add to the frying pan on a medium-low heat with an extra tbsp of olive oil. Cook for 1 minute. Season with salt and pepper.
- Drain the chickpeas and add to the pan, cooking for another 2 minutes.
- Rinse the spinach or rocket. Tear up roughly and add to the pan. Stir into the mix for 1 minute as it wilts.
- Zest the lemon directly into the pan then squeeze its juice in, watching out for any pips. Add the butter if using. Return the bread to the pan. Turn the heat off.
- Drain the pasta, reserving half a cup of cooking water. Add the pasta to the pan along with some cooking water to loosen the mix up.
- Grate the cheddar into a bowl.
- Serve the pasta in bowls with the grated cheddar and the bottle of olive oil on the table to add as you like.

Lightning Source UK Ltd.
Milton Keynes UK
UKHW050524090920
369560UK00009B/178